D0206583

Gender
Second Edition

Gender
In World Perspective

Second Edition
Raewyn Connell

polity

Copyright © Raewyn Connell 2009

The right of Raewyn Connell to be identified as Author of this Work has been asserted in accordance with the UK Copyright, Designs and Patents Act 1988.

First published in 2009 by Polity Press
Reprinted 2009, 2010 (three times)

Polity Press
65 Bridge Street
Cambridge CB2 1UR, UK

Polity Press
350 Main Street
Malden, MA 02148, USA

All rights reserved. Except for the quotation of short passages for the purpose of criticism and review, no part of this publication may be reproduced, stored in a retrieval system, or transmitted, in any form or by any means, electronic, mechanical, photocopying, recording or otherwise, without the prior permission of the publisher.

ISBN-13: 978-0-7456-4567-4
ISBN-13: 978-0-7456-4568-1(paperback)

A catalogue record for this book is available from the British Library.

Typeset in 10 on 12 pt Sabon
by SNP Best-set Typesetter Ltd, Hong Kong
Printed and bound in Great Britain by the MPG Books Group

The publisher has used its best endeavours to ensure that the URLs for external websites referred to in this book are correct and active at the time of going to press. However, the publisher has no responsibility for the websites and can make no guarantee that a site will remain live or that the content is or will remain appropriate.

Every effort has been made to trace all copyright holders, but if any have been inadvertently overlooked the publishers will be pleased to include any necessary credits in any subsequent reprint or edition.

For further information on Polity, visit our website: www.politybooks.com.

In memory of
Pam Benton
1942–1997

She, who had Here so much essentiall joy
As no chance could distract, much lesse destroy;
. . . she to Heaven is gone,
Who made this world in some proportion
A heaven, and here, became unto us all,
Joy, (as our joyes admit) essentiall.

Contents

Preface

Gender is a key dimension of personal life, social relations and culture. It is an arena in which we face difficult practical issues about justice, identity and even survival.

Gender is also a topic on which there is a great deal of prejudice, myth and outright falsehood. Many people believe that women and men are psychologically opposites, that men are more intelligent than women, that men are naturally violent, or that gender patterns never change. All these beliefs are factually wrong. Many people imagine masculinity, femininity and gender relations only in terms of their own local gender system. They miss the vast diversity of gender patterns across cultures and down history.

Research and theory in the human sciences provide vital tools for dispelling prejudices and understanding the real issues. Therefore this book tries to present an accessible, research-based, globally informed and theoretically coherent account of gender.

For people new to the study of gender, I introduce key examples of gender research, describe the main findings on key topics, and provide a map of debates and ideas. For people already working on gender issues, I propose an integrated approach that links issues ranging from the body and personality difference to the global economy and world peace. To understand these questions, we have to move across conventional boundaries between academic disciplines. Accordingly, the book draws on a spectrum of the human sciences, from psychology and sociology to political science, cultural studies, education and history.

Psychological and social sciences are relatively new forms of knowledge. Based on both empirical research and conceptual reasoning, the human sciences seek to build knowledge over time. This requires us to be energetic in seeking out new information, and at the same time open to critique and willing to change obsolete ideas. When these processes work well, the human sciences provide a powerful way of understanding our social life.

Modern research on gender was triggered by the women's movement for gender equality. There is a simple reason for this: most gender orders, around the world, privilege men and disadvantage women. That is a basic fact; yet the details are not simple. There are different forms of privilege and disadvantage, ranging from pure symbolism to brutal violence. The degree of gender inequality varies from place to place. The costs of privilege may be high. Even the definition of who is a man and who is a woman can be contested.

Gender issues are about men quite as much as they are about women. There is now extensive research and public debate about masculinities, fatherhood, men's movements, men's violence, boys' education, men's health and men's involvement in achieving gender equality. In this book I have woven this research systematically into the picture of gender.

I have also taken account of the fact that gender reform and gender science are world-wide. We must acknowledge the creative role of intellectuals from Europe and North America in understanding gender problems. But the view from the global North is not the only possible view of the world. Therefore I give considerable attention to gender research and theory in countries outside the global metropole, places as diverse as Latvia, Chile, Australia, western and southern Africa, and Japan.

We particularly need an international approach to gender studies now. The deepening of economic interdependence, the creation of global media, the interlinking of political systems, all of which are now called 'globalization', have powerful implications for gender. In front of our eyes, new gender orders are being created: through labour migration, in transnational corporations and global markets, in transnational media and international state structures. New identities and movements are created, and knowledge about them circulates globally.

The world faces new and urgent issues about gender. Indeed, a whole new realm of gender politics is emerging, with sharp questions about human rights, economic equality, environmental impacts, relations between generations, violence and well-being.

If the emerging gender orders are to be just, peaceful and humane – which is by no means guaranteed – we need well-founded knowledge and sophisticated understanding of gender issues. To produce this knowledge and understanding must be a shared project around the globe. I hope this book will contribute to this work. Its first edition, written in English, has been translated into Italian, Greek, Chinese, Swedish and

Japanese. This second edition expands the coverage of international research and theory and I hope will continue the global dialogue.

A book that tries to synthesize knowledge across a broad field of study rests on the labour of many people – researchers, theorists, social movement activists, and the many people who contribute to research projects as 'subjects'. The Women's Liberation movement emphasized the collective production of ideas and I have tried to acknowledge that in the text.

At the same time, any book reflects the author's personal background. I am a professional social scientist with a long experience of research and teaching, some of it directly about gender but some of it also about class, education, child development and social theory. I have lived most of my life in Australia, a rich country in the global periphery, the product of British settler colonialism. I read several languages, but all are European-derived, and this limits my knowledge of global research and debate. I have tried to expand this knowledge through translations and travel. I have visited nearly thirty other countries and talked with social scientists in most of them.

I have a personal, not just intellectual, engagement in these issues. Much of my research has been designed to help reforms such as gender equality in the public service, or to serve causes such as AIDS prevention. I have a lively interest in the gender politics of relationships because my partner and I debated them, and lived them, for twenty-nine years. I have a close interest in parent/child relations because I am a parent, for years a sole parent. My personal experience of gender has involved strong contradictions. Being a transsexual woman has, perhaps, given me some empathy across the conventional gender divide.

Most of my intellectual debts are acknowledged in the text. I owe particular thanks to: John Fisher for research assistance; Christabel Draffin for clerical assistance; Patricia Selkirk for expert advice on biology; Carol Hagemann-White for posing crucial questions about theory and politics; Robert Morrell, Ulla Müller, Taga Futoshi and Teresa Valdés for opening cultural worlds for me; Toni Schofield for demanding relevance; Lin Walker for demanding coherence; Kirsten Gomard for demanding precision. I thank all these people, and other friends, for providing vital encouragement and support. Kylie Benton-Connell has provided support and inspiration in more ways than I can say. The book is dedicated to the memory of her mother, my partner, Pam Benton. The epigraph at the start of the book is from Pam's favourite poet, John Donne, and can be found in the poem 'The second Anniversarie'.

Raewyn Connell
University of Sydney

1

The question of gender

Noticing gender

One night a year, the attention of the TV-watching world is focused on Hollywood's most spectacular event, the Oscar award ceremony. Famous people are driven up in limousines in front of an enthusiastic crowd, and in a blizzard of camera flashes they walk into the auditorium – the men in tuxedos striding easily, the women going cautiously because they are wearing low-cut gowns and high-heeled shoes. As the evening wears on, awards are given out for film score, camera work, script writing, direction, best foreign film, and so on. But in the categories that concern the people you see on screen when you go to the movies, there are *two* awards given: best actor *and* best actress; best supporting actor *and* best supporting actress.

On my way to work in the morning, I pass a news-agency that displays posters for the week's mass-circulation magazines. Almost every poster shows a young woman, usually blonde, dangerously thin, heavily made up, very pretty, and not doing anything. These women are known in the media trade as 'celebs'. Deeper in the shop are magazines about motor bikes, cars, sport, power boats and fishing. These may also have pictures of blonde young women on the cover, in rather more pornographic poses than the ones outside, but also show men, who will be riding the bikes, driving the cars and boats, and catching stupendous fish.

In September 2007 my home town of Sydney, noted for its excellent fish, hosted an international gathering called the Asia-Pacific Economic Cooperation (APEC) forum. The centre of the city was blocked off by heavy concrete barriers, wire, and rows of police drafted in from all over the state. Behind the wire, protected from the annoyance of the townspeople, was a formidable concentration of global power. Those present included Mr Hu, the president of China; Mr Putin, the president of Russia; Mr Bush, the president of the United States; Mr Yudhoyono, the president of Indonesia; as well as minor figures like Mr Howard, the prime minister of Australia. At the end of this conference there is traditionally a group photograph of the leaders wearing folkloric shirts from the host country; in this case, folkloric raincoats. The photograph, taken in front of the Sydney Opera House, shows eighteen middle-aged men, trying to hide their embarrassment, and three women.

This balance is hardly unusual. If Hillary Clinton had won the Democratic Party nomination, she would have become the first woman major-party candidate for president in the 200-year history of the United States. There has never been a woman head of government in modern Russia, China, France, Brazil, Japan, Egypt, Nigeria, South Africa or Mexico, and only one each in the history of Germany, Britain, India and Indonesia. Every secretary-general of the United Nations and every head of the World Bank has been a man. In the same year as the APEC forum, 2007, statistics from the Inter-Parliamentary Union showed that 82.5 per cent of members of the world's parliaments were men.

Among cabinet ministers, the predominance of men is even higher. In 2005, just two countries in the world had women making up half of a national cabinet (Sweden and Spain). More typical figures for the representation of women were 14 per cent (United States, Ecuador), 10 per cent (Algeria), 8 per cent (Italy, Argentina), 6 per cent (China) and 0 per cent (Saudi Arabia, Russia). The few women who do get to this level are usually given the job of running welfare or education ministries. Men keep control of taxation, investment, technology, international relations, police and the military.

What is true of politics is also true of business. Of the top 200 businesses listed on the Australian stock exchange in 2007 (including those that publish the mass-circulation magazines), just 5 had a woman as Chief Executive Officer (CEO). Of the 500 giant international corporations listed in *Fortune* magazine's 'Global 500' in 2007, just 10 had a woman CEO. Such figures are usually presented by saying that women now form 2 per cent of the top business leadership around the world. It's more informative to say that men compose 98 per cent of that leadership.

Women are a substantial part of the paid workforce, lower down the hierarchy. They are mostly concentrated in service jobs – clerical work, call centres, cleaning, serving food, and professions connected with caring for the young and the sick, i.e. teaching and nursing. In some parts of the world, women are also valued as industrial workers, for instance in microprocessor plants, because of their supposedly 'nimble fingers'. Though the detailed division between men's and women's work varies in different parts of the world, it is common for men to predominate in heavy industry, mining, transport, indeed in most jobs that involve any machinery except a sewing machine. World-wide, men are a large majority of the workforce in management, accountancy, law and technical professions such as engineering and computing.

Behind the paid workforce is another form of work – unpaid domestic and care work. In all contemporary societies for which we have statistics, women do most of the cleaning, cooking and sewing, most of the work of looking after children, and almost all of the work of caring for babies. (If you don't think this is work, you haven't done it yet.) This work is often associated with a cultural definition of women as caring, gentle, self-sacrificing and industrious, i.e. as good mothers. Being a good father is rarely associated with cutting school lunches and wiping babies' bottoms – though there are now interesting attempts to promote what in Mexico has been called 'paternidad afectiva', i.e. emotionally engaged fatherhood. Normally, fathers are supposed to be decision-makers and breadwinners, to consume the services provided by women and represent the family in the outside world.

Women are less likely to be out in the public world than men, and, when they are, have fewer resources. In almost all parts of the world, men are more likely to have a paid job. The world 'economic activity rate' for women has crept up, but is still just over two-thirds of the rate for men. The main exceptions are Scandinavia and parts of west Africa, where women's relative labour force participation rates are unusually high. But in some Arab states women's participation rates are one-quarter the rate for men, and in much of south Asia and Latin America they are about half the rate for men.

Once in the workforce, how do wages compare? Thirty years after the United Nations adopted the Convention on the Elimination of All Forms of Discrimination against Women, nowhere in the world are women's earned incomes equal to men's. They reach 81 per cent of men's earned incomes in Sweden; but more typical figures are: 64 per cent of men's incomes in France, 63 per cent in the United States, 55 per cent in Ukraine, 46 per cent in Indonesia, 39 per cent in Mexico.

Therefore, most women in the world, especially women with children, are economically dependent on men. Some men believe that women who are dependent on them must be their property. This is a common scenario in domestic violence: when dependent women don't conform to demands from their husband or boyfriend, they are beaten. This creates a dilemma for the women, which is very familiar to domestic violence services. They can stay, and put themselves and their children at high risk of further violence; or go, and lose their home, economic support and status in the community. If they go, certain husbands are so infuriated that they pursue and kill the wives and even the children.

Men are not beaten up by their spouses so often, but men are at risk of other forms of violence. Most assaults reported to the police, in countries with good statistics on the matter, are by men on other men. Some men are beaten, indeed some are murdered, simply because they are thought to be homosexual; and some of this violence comes from the police. Most of the prisoners in gaols are men. In the United States, which has the biggest prison system in the world, in mid-2007 there was a prison population of 1.59 million, and 92.8 per cent were men. Most deaths in combat are men, because men make up the vast majority of the troops in armies and militias. Most industrial accidents involve men, because men are most of the workforce in dangerous industries such as construction and mining.

Men are involved disproportionately in violence partly because they have been prepared for it. Though patterns of child rearing differ between cultures, the situation in Australia is not unusual. Australian boys are steered towards competitive sports such as football, where physical dominance is celebrated, from an early age – by their fathers, by schools and by the mass media. Boys also come under peer pressure to show bravery and toughness, and learn to fear being classified as 'sissies' or 'poofters' (a local term meaning effeminate or homosexual). Being capable of violence becomes a social resource. Working-class boys, who don't have the other resources that will lead to a professional career, become the main recruits into jobs that require the use of force: police, the military, private security, blue-collar crime and professional sport. It is mainly young women who are recruited into the jobs that repair the consequences of violence: nursing, psychology and social work.

So far, I have listed an assortment of facts, about mass media, about politics and business, about families and about growing up. Are these random? Modern thought about gender starts with the recognition that they are not. These facts form a pattern; they make sense when seen as parts of the overall gender arrangement, which I will call the gender order, of contemporary societies.

To notice the existence of the gender order is easy; to understand it is not. Conflicting theories of gender now exist, and some problems about gender are genuinely difficult to resolve. Yet we now have a rich resource of knowledge about gender, derived from decades of research, and a fund of practical experience from gender reform. We now have a better basis for understanding gender issues than any previous generation had.

Understanding gender

In everyday life we take gender for granted. We instantly recognize a person as a man or woman, girl or boy. We arrange everyday business around the distinction. Conventional marriages require one of each. Mixed doubles tennis requires two of each, but most sports require one kind at a time.

Next to Oscar night, the most popular television broadcast in the world is said to be the American Super Bowl, another strikingly gendered event: large armoured men crash into each other while chasing a pointed leather bladder, and thin women in short skirts dance and smile in the pauses. Most of us cannot crash or dance nearly so well, but we do our best in other ways. As women or men we slip our feet into differently shaped shoes, button our shirts on opposite sides, get our heads clipped by different hairdressers, buy our pants in separate shops, and take them off in separate toilets.

These arrangements are so familiar that they can seem part of the order of nature. Belief that gender distinction is 'natural' makes it scandalous when people don't follow the pattern – for instance, when people of the same gender fall in love with each other. So homosexuality is frequently declared 'unnatural' and bad.

But if having sex with a fellow-woman or a fellow-man is unnatural, why have a law against it? We don't provide penalties for violating the third law of thermodynamics. Anti-gay ordinances in United States' cities, police harassment of gay men in Senegal, the criminalization of women's adultery in Islamic Sharia law, the imprisonment of transsexual women for violating public order – such things only make sense because these matters are *not* fixed by nature.

These events are part of an enormous social effort to channel people's behaviour. Ideas about gender-appropriate behaviour are constantly being circulated, not only by legislators but also by priests, parents, teachers, advertisers, retail mall owners, talk-show hosts and disc jockeys. Events like Oscar night and the Super Bowl are not just consequences of our ideas about gender difference. They also help to *create* gender difference, by displays of exemplary masculinities and femininities.

Being a man or a woman, then, is not a pre-determined state. It is a *becoming*, a condition actively under construction. The pioneering French feminist Simone de Beauvoir put this in a classic phrase: 'One is not born, but rather becomes, a woman.' Though the positions of women and men are not simply parallel, the principle is also true for men: one is not born masculine, but has to become a man.

This process is often discussed as the development of 'gender identity'. I have some doubts about this concept (see chapter 6), but it will serve for the moment as a name for the sense of belonging to a gender category. Identity includes our ideas of what that belonging means, what kind of person we are, in consequence of being a woman or a man. These ideas are not presented to the baby as a package at the beginning of life. They develop (there is some controversy about exactly when), and are filled out in detail over a long period of years, as we grow up.

As de Beauvoir further recognized, this business of becoming a gendered person follows many different paths, involves many tensions and ambiguities, and sometimes produces unstable results. Part of the mystery of gender is how a pattern that on the surface appears so stark and rigid, on close examination turns out so complex and uncertain.

So we cannot think of womanhood or manhood as fixed by nature. But neither should we think of them as simply imposed from outside, by social norms or pressure from authorities. People construct *themselves* as masculine or feminine. We claim a place in the gender order – or respond to the place we have been given – by the way we conduct ourselves in everyday life.

Most people do this willingly, and often enjoy the gender polarity. Yet gender ambiguities are not rare. There are masculine women and feminine men. There are women in love with other women, and men in love with other men. There are women who are heads of households, and men who bring up children. There are women who are soldiers and men who are nurses. Sometimes the development of 'gender identity' results in intermediate, blended or sharply contradictory patterns, for which we use terms like 'effeminate', 'camp', 'queer' and 'transgender'.

Psychological research suggests that the great majority of us combine masculine and feminine characteristics, in varying blends, rather than being all one or all the other. Gender ambiguity can be an object of fascination and desire, as well as disgust. Gender impersonations are familiar in both popular and high culture, from the cross-dressed actors of Shakespeare's stage to drag movies like *Priscilla, Queen of the Desert*.

There is certainly enough gender blending to provoke heated opposition from movements dedicated to re-establishing 'the traditional family', 'true femininity' or 'real masculinity'. By 1988 the Pope had become so concerned that he issued an Apostolic Letter, *On the Dignity and Vocation of Women*, reminding everyone that women were created for motherhood and their functions should not get mixed up with those of men. The efforts to maintain strong divisions are themselves strong evidence that the boundaries are none too stable.

But these are not just boundaries, they are also inequalities. Most churches and mosques are run exclusively by men, and this is part of a larger pattern. Most corporate wealth is in the hands of men, most big institutions are run by men, and most science and technology is controlled by men. In many countries, including some with very large populations, women are less likely than men to have been taught to read. For instance, recent adult literacy rates in India stood at 73 per cent for men and 48 per cent for women; in Nigeria, 78 per cent for men and 60 per cent for women. On a world scale, two-thirds of illiterate people are women. In countries like the United States, Australia, Italy and Turkey, middle-class women have gained full access to higher education and have made inroads into middle management and professions. But even in those countries many informal barriers operate to keep the very top levels of power and wealth mostly a world of men.

There is also unequal respect. In many situations, including the cheerleaders at the football game, women are treated as marginal to the main action, or as the objects of men's desire. Whole genres of humour – bimbo jokes, woman-driver jokes, mother-in-law jokes – are based on contempt for women's triviality and stupidity. A whole industry, ranging from heavy pornography and prostitution to soft-core advertising, markets women's bodies as objects of consumption by men. Equal-opportunity reforms in the workplace often run into a refusal by men to be under the authority of a woman. Not only do most religions prevent women from holding major religious office, they often treat women symbolically as a source of defilement for men.

Though men in general benefit from the inequalities of the gender order, they do not benefit equally. Indeed, many pay a considerable price. Boys and men who depart from dominant definitions of masculinity because they are gay, effeminate or simply wimpish are often subject to verbal abuse and discrimination, and are sometimes the targets of violence. Men who conform to dominant definitions of masculinity may also pay a price. Research on men's health shows that men have a higher rate of industrial accidents than women, have a higher rate of death by violence, tend to eat a worse diet and drink more alcohol, and (not surprisingly) have more sporting injuries. In 2005, the life expectancy for men in the United States was calculated at seventy-five years, compared with eighty years for women. In Russia, after the restoration of capitalism, life expectancy for men was fifty-nine years, compared with seventy-two years for women.

Gender arrangements are thus, at the same time, sources of pleasure, recognition and identity, and sources of injustice and harm. This means that gender is inherently political – but it also means the politics can be complicated and difficult.

Inequality and oppression in the gender order have repeatedly led to demands for reform. Movements for change include campaigns for women's right to vote, and for women's presence in anti-colonial movements and representation in independent governments; campaigns for equal pay, for women's right to own property, for homosexual law reform, for women's trade unionism, for equal employment opportunity, for reproductive rights, for the human rights of transsexual men and women and transgender people; and campaigns against discrimination in education, against sexist media, against rape and domestic violence.

Political campaigns resisting some of these changes, or seeking counter-changes, have also arisen. The scene of gender politics currently includes anti-gay campaigns, anti-abortion ('pro-life') campaigns, a spectrum of men's movements, and a complex international debate about links between Western feminism and Western cultural dominance in the world.

In this history, the feminist and gay movements of the 1960s–1970s were pivotal. They did not reach all their political goals, but they had a profound cultural impact. They called attention to a whole realm of human reality that was poorly understood, and thus created a demand for understanding as well as action. This was the historical take-off point of contemporary gender research. Political practice launched a deep change – which increasingly seems like a revolution – in human knowledge.

This book is an attempt to map this revolution. It describes the terrain revealed by gender politics and gender research, introduces the debates about how to understand it and change it, and offers solutions to some of the problems raised.

In chapter 2, I discuss five notable examples of gender research, to show how the broad issues just discussed take shape in specific investigations. Chapter 3 discusses theories and models of gender, and the intellectuals who produce them. Chapter 4 turns to the issue of 'difference', the extent of sex differences, and the way bodies and society interact. This requires an account of gender as a social structure, which I present in chapter 5, exploring the different dimensions of gender and the process of historical change. Chapter 6 discusses gender on the small scale, in personal life, and looks at the emerging debate about gender transition. Chapter 7 moves to the large scale, looking at gender relations in institutions and world society. Chapter 8 is a kind of synthesis, focused on gender politics, considering what is at stake in movements for change. Here I raise questions about both the micro-politics of personal life, and the large-scale politics of institutions and movements, ending with a discussion of gender politics in world society.

Defining gender

As a new awareness of issues developed, a new terminology was needed. From the 1970s, the term 'gender' has become common in English-language discussions to describe the whole field (though it has never been universally accepted). The term was borrowed from grammar. Ultimately it comes from an ancient word-root meaning 'to produce' (cf. 'generate'), which gave rise to words in many languages meaning 'kind' or 'class' (e.g. 'genus'). In grammar 'gender' came to refer to the specific distinction between classes of nouns 'corresponding more or less' – as the nineteenth-century *Oxford English Dictionary* primly noted – 'to distinctions of sex (and absence of sex) in the objects denoted'.

Grammar suggests how such distinctions permeate cultures. In Indo-European and Semitic languages, nouns, adjectives and pronouns may be distinguishable as feminine, masculine, neuter or common gender. Not only the words for species that reproduce sexually may be gendered, but also many other words for objects, concepts and states of mind. English is a relatively un-gendered language, but English speakers still call a ship 'she', and even an oil well ('she's going to blow!').

Language is an important aspect of gender, but does not provide a consistent framework for understanding it. German, for instance, has 'die Frau' (the woman) feminine, but 'das Mädchen' (the girl) neuter, because all words with such diminutives are neuter. Terror is feminine in French ('la terreur'), but masculine in German ('der Terror'). Other languages, including Chinese, Japanese and Yoruba, do not make gender distinctions through word forms at all. A great deal also depends on how a language is used, not just its grammar. A relatively non-gendered language can still be used to name gender positions and express opinions on gender issues. On the other hand, there are many communities where certain words or tones of voice are specifically thought to belong to men or women, or to express the speaker's masculinity or femininity.

Most discussions of gender in society emphasize a dichotomy. Starting from a presumed biological divide between male and female, they define gender as the social or psychological difference that corresponds to that divide, builds on it or is caused by it.

In its most common usage, then, the term 'gender' means the cultural difference of women from men, based on the biological division between male and female. Dichotomy and difference are the substance of the idea. Men are from Mars, women are from Venus.

There are decisive objections to such a definition.

- Human life does not simply divide into two realms, nor does human character divide into two types. Our images of gender are often dichotomous, but the reality is not. Abundant evidence will be seen throughout this book.
- A definition in terms of difference means that where we cannot see difference, we cannot see gender. With such a definition we could not recognize the gendered character of lesbian or homosexual desire (based on gender similarity). We would be thrown into confusion by research which found only small psychological differences between women and men, which would seem to imply that gender had evaporated. (See chapter 4.)
- A definition based on dichotomy excludes the differences among women, and among men, from the concept of gender. But there are such differences that are highly relevant to the pattern of relations between women and men – for instance, the difference between violent and non-violent masculinities. (See chapter 6.)
- Any definition in terms of personal characteristics excludes processes which lie beyond the individual person. Large-scale social processes are based on the *shared* capacities of women and men more than on their differences. The creation of goods and services in a modern economy is based on shared capacities and cooperative labour – yet the products are often strongly gendered, and the wealth generated is distributed in highly gendered ways, so this must be included in the analysis of gender.

The development of social science has provided a solution to these difficulties. The key is to move from a focus on difference to a focus on *relations*. Gender is, above all, a matter of the social relations within which individuals and groups act.

Enduring or widespread patterns among social relations are what social theory calls 'structures'. In this sense, gender must be understood as a social structure. It is not an expression of biology, nor a fixed dichotomy in human life or character. It is a pattern in our social arrangements, and in the everyday activities or practices which those arrangements govern.

Gender is a social structure, but of a particular kind. Gender involves a specific relationship with bodies. This is recognized in the common-sense definition of gender as an expression of natural difference, the bodily distinction of male from female. We certainly are one of the species that reproduce sexually rather than vegetatively (though cloning may change that soon!). Some aspects of our anatomy are specialized for this purpose, and many biological processes in our bodies are affected by it (see chapter 4). What is wrong with this definition is not the attention to bodies, nor the concern with sexual reproduction, but the squeezing of biological complexity and adaptability into a stark dichotomy, and the idea that cultural patterns simply 'express' bodily difference.

Sometimes cultural patterns do express bodily difference, for instance when they celebrate first menstruation as a distinction between girl and woman. But often they do more than that, or less than that. In relation to the distinction of male from female bodies, social practices sometimes exaggerate (e.g. maternity clothes), sometimes deny (many employment practices), sometimes mythologize (computer games), sometimes complicate ('third gender' customs). So we cannot say that social arrangements routinely 'express' biological difference.

But we can say that, in all of these cases, society *addresses* bodies and *deals with* reproductive processes and differences among bodies. There is no fixed 'biological base' for the social process of gender. Rather, there is an arena in which bodies are brought into social processes, in which our social conduct *does something* with reproductive difference. I will call this the 'reproductive arena'.

This allows us to define gender in a way that solves the paradoxes of 'difference'. *Gender is the structure of social relations that centres on the reproductive arena, and the set of practices that bring reproductive distinctions between bodies into social processes.* To put it informally, gender concerns the way human society deals with human bodies and their continuity, and the many consequences of that 'dealing' in our personal lives and our collective fate. The terms used in this definition are explained more fully in chapters 4 and 5.

This definition has important consequences; here are some. Gender, like other social structures, is multi-dimensional; it is not just about identity, or just about work, or just about power, or just about sexuality, but all of these things at once. Gender patterns may differ strikingly from one cultural context to another, but are still 'gender'. Gender arrangements are reproduced socially (not biologically) by the power of structures to shape individual action, so they often appear unchanging. Yet gender arrangements are in fact always changing, as human practice creates new situations and as structures develop crisis tendencies. Finally, gender had a beginning and may have an end. Each of these points will be explored later in the book.

Note on sources

Most of the statistics mentioned in this chapter, such as income, economic activity rates and literacy, can be found in the United Nations Development Programme's *Human Development Report 2007/2008*

(2007; see list of references at back of book), or on-line tables regularly published by the United Nations Statistics Division. Figures on parliamentary representation and numbers of ministers are from Inter-Parliamentary Union (2007), and on managers, from Glass Ceiling Commission (1995) and *Fortune*, 23 July 2007. Sources of information on men's health can be found in Schofield et al. (2000). The quotation on 'woman' is from de Beauvoir's *The Second Sex* (1949: 295). Definitions and etymology of the word 'gender' are in *The Oxford English Dictionary*, vol. IV (Oxford: Clarendon Press, 1933), 100.

2

Gender research:
five examples

Often a complex problem is best approached through specifics, and the results of research are best understood by looking at particular research projects. In this chapter I discuss five notable studies of gender issues published in recent decades. They come from five continents. Three focus on everyday life in local settings – a school, a workplace, a personal life. One deals with gender change in a great historical transition, and another with gender reform at a face-to-face level. Though they deal with very different questions, they reveal some of the main concerns of gender research in general.

Case 1. The play of gender in school life

One of the most difficult tasks in social research is to take a situation that everyone thinks they understand, and illuminate it in new ways. This is what the US ethnographer Barrie Thorne achieves in her subtly observed and highly readable book about school life, *Gender Play* (1993).

At the time Thorne started her work, children were not much discussed in gender research. When they were mentioned, it was usually assumed that they were being 'socialized' into gender roles, in a top-down transmission from the adult world. It was assumed that there are two sex roles, a male one and a female one, with boys and girls getting separately inducted into the norms and expectations of the appropriate one. This idea was based on a certain amount of research using paper-and-pencil questionnaires, but not on much actual observation of gender in children's lives.

Thorne did that observation. Her book is based on fieldwork in two elementary (primary) schools in different parts of the United States. She spent eight months in one, three months in another, hanging about in classrooms, hallways and playgrounds, talking to everyone and watching the way the children interacted with each other and with their teachers in work and play.

Ethnography as a method sounds easy, but in practice is hard to do well. Part of the problem is the mass of information an observer can get from just a single day 'in the field'. You need to know what you are looking for. But you also need to be open to new experiences and new information, able to see things that you did not expect to see.

As an observer, Thorne was certainly interested in transmission from older people, in the ways children pick up the details of how to do gender. Her funniest (and perhaps also saddest) chapter is called 'Lip gloss and "goin' with"', about how pre-adolescent children learn the techniques of teenage flirting and dating. She was also interested in the differences between the girls' and the boys' informal interactions – the games they played, spaces they used, words they spoke, and so on.

But Thorne was able to see beyond the patterns described in conventional gender models. She became aware how much these models predisposed an observer to look for difference. She began to pay attention not only to the moments in school life when the boys and girls separated, but also to the moments when they came together. She began to think of gender difference as *situational*, as created in some situations and ignored or overridden in others. Even in recess-time games, where the girls and boys were usually clustered in separate parts of the playground, they sometimes moved into mixed activities without any emphasis on difference. There were many 'relaxed cross-sex interactions' in the school's daily routine. Clearly, the boys and girls were not permanently in separate spheres, nor permanently enacting opposite 'sex roles'.

Recognizing this fact opened up a number of other issues. What were the situations where gender was emphasized or de-emphasized? Thorne noticed that, though teachers sometimes emphasized gender – for instance, arranging a classroom learning game with the girls competing against the boys – most teacher-controlled activities de-emphasized gender. This is true, for instance, of the commonest teaching technique in schools, the 'talk-and-chalk' method where the teacher at the front of the room demands the attention of all the pupils to an exposition of some lesson that they all have to learn. In this situation the basic division is between teacher and taught, not between groups of pupils; so girls and boys are in the same boat.

Next, how did the children establish gender difference when they did emphasize it? Thorne began to identify a kind of activity she called 'borderwork': 'When gender boundaries are activated, the loose aggregations "boys and girls" consolidates into "the boys" and "the girls" as separate and reified groups. In the process, categories of identity that on other occasions have minimal relevance for interaction become the basis of separate collectivities' (1993: 65).

There are different kinds of borderwork in a primary school. One of the most interesting is chasing, a kind of game that is sometimes very fluid and sometimes not. I remember a chasing game at my primary school, a rather intimidating game called 'cocky-laura', which was extremely rule-bound. One of the implicit rules was that only boys could play, because the girls were forbidden by the school to be in the part of the playground where a big eucalyptus tree stood, which was one of the bases for the game. In the schools Thorne studied, boys and girls could play together, and often chased each other, playing 'girls-chase-the-boys' and 'boys-chase-the-girls'. Indeed the one game would often merge into the other, as the chased turned around and became the chasers. Thorne notes that often boys chased boys, or girls chased girls, but these patterns attracted little attention or discussion. However girls-chasing-boys/boys-chasing-girls often resulted in lively discussion and excitement. It was a situation in which

> Gender terms blatantly override individual identities, especially in references to the other team ('Help, a girl's chasin' me'; 'C'mon Sarah, let's get that boy'; 'Tony, help save me from the girls'). Individuals may call for help from, or offer help to, others of their gender. And in acts of treason, they may grab someone from their team and turn them over to the other side. For example, in an elaborate chasing scene among a group of Ashton third-graders, Ryan grabbed Billy from behind, wrestling him to the ground. 'Hey girls, get 'im', Ryan called. (1993: 69)

Thorne's observation of children might alert us to parallel processes among adults. Borderwork is constantly being done to mark gender boundaries, if not by chasing then by jokes, dress, forms of speech, etc. Gender difference is not something that simply exists. It is something that happens, and must be made to happen; something, also, that can be unmade, altered, made less important.

The games in which the children make gender happen do something more. When the girls chase the boys and the boys chase the girls, they seem to be acting equally, and in some respects they are – but not in all respects. For a rough-and-tumble version of the chasing game is more common among the boys. Boys normally control more of the playground space than the girls do, more often invade girls' groups and disrupt the girls' activities than the girls disrupt theirs. That is to say, the boys more often make an aggressive move and a claim to power, in the limited sense that children can do this.

In the symbolic realm, too, the boys claim power. They treat girls as a source of contamination or pollution, for instance calling low-status boys 'girls' or pushing them next to the space occupied by girls. The girls do not treat the boys that way. Girls are more often defined as giving the imaginary disease called 'cooties', and low-status girls may get called 'cootie queens'. A version of cooties played in one of the schools is called 'girl stain'. All these may seem small matters. But, as Thorne remarks, 'recoiling from physical proximity with another person and their belongings because they are perceived as contaminating is a powerful statement of social distance and claimed superiority' (1993: 75).

So there is an asymmetry in the situations of boys and girls, which is reflected in differences among the boys and among the girls. Some boys often interrupt the girls' games, other boys do not. Some boys have higher status, others have lower. Some of the girls move earlier than others into 'romance'. By fourth grade, homophobic insults – such as calling another boy a 'fag' – are becoming common among the boys, most of whom learn that this word is a way of expressing hostility before they know what its sexual meaning is. At the same time, however, physical contact among the boys is becoming less common – they are learning to fear, or be suspicious of, displays of affection. In short, the children are beginning to show something of the differentiation of gender patterns, and the gender and sexual hierarchies, that are familiar among adults.

There is much more in Thorne's fascinating book, including a humorous and insightful discussion of what it is like for an adult to do research among children. For me, the most important lesson her book teaches is about these American children's *agency* in learning gender. They are not passively 'socialized' into a sex role. They are, of course, learning things from the adult world around them: lessons about available identities, lessons about performance, and – regrettably – lessons about hatred. But they do this actively, and on their own terms. They find gender interesting and sometimes exciting. They move into and out of gender-based groupings. They sometimes shore up, and sometimes move across, gender boundaries. They even play with and against the gender dichotomy itself. Gender is important in their world, but it is important as a human issue that they deal with, not as a fixed framework that reduces them to puppets.

Case 2. Manhood and the mines

In the late nineteenth century, the fabulous wealth of the largest gold deposit in the world began to be exploited by the Dutch and British colonists in South Africa. The Witwatersrand (Whitewater Ridge) gold deposits were immense. But the ore was low-grade, so huge volumes had to be processed. And the main deposits lay far below the high plateau of the Transvaal, so the mines had to go deep. The first wild gold-rushes soon turned into an organized industry dominated by large companies, with a total workforce of hundreds of thousands.

Because the price of gold on the world market was fixed, the companies' profitability depended on keeping labour costs down. Thus the industry needed a large but low-paid workforce for demanding and dangerous conditions underground. To colonial entrepreneurs, the answer was obvious: indigenous men. So Black African men, recruited from many parts of South Africa and even beyond, became the main labour force of the gold industry – and have remained so ever since.

Over a twenty-year period, T. Dunbar Moodie worked with a series of partners to document the experience of men who made up this labour force, a key group in South Africa's history. Their story is told in his book *Going for Gold* (1994). Moodie studied the company archives and government records, directed participant-observation studies, interviewed miners, mine executives and women in the 'townships' where Black workers lived. A key moment came when one of his collaborators, Vivienne Ndatshe, interviewed forty *retired* miners in their home country, Pondoland (near the south-eastern coast). Her interviews revealed aspects of the miners' experience which changed the picture of migrant labour profoundly.

Because the mines were large-scale industrial enterprises owned by European capital, it had been easy to think of the mineworkers as 'proletarians' on the model of European urban industrial workers. But the reality was different. The racial structure of the South African workforce – Whites as managers, Blacks providing the labour – might have kept labour costs down, but also created a barrier behind which the mineworkers could sustain cultures of their own, and exercise some informal control over their work. Most lived in all-male compounds near the mines, where they had to create their own social lives.

When the men signed on with recruiting agents – generally on contracts lasting four months to two years – and travelled hundreds of kilometres to the mines, they did not take families with them and did not intend to become city dwellers. This was not just because the wages were too low to support families in the cash economy of the cities. More importantly, the mineworkers mostly came from areas with a small-holder agricultural economy, such as Pondoland. They kept their links to that economy, and intended to return to it.

For most of them, the point of earning wages at the mine was to subsidize rural households run by their families, or to accumulate resources that would allow them to establish new rural households on their return – buying cattle, financing marriages, etc. Being the wise and respected head of a self-sufficient homestead was the ideal of 'manhood' to which Mpondo migrant workers (alongside others) subscribed. The mine work was a means to this end.

This situation led to gender practices very different from those of the conventional European breadwinner/housewife couple. First, the men working at the mines and living in the compounds had to provide their own domestic labour, and, if sexually active, find new sexual partners. Some went to women working in nearby towns. Others created sexual and domestic partnerships, known as 'mine marriages', between older and younger men in the compounds. In such an arrangement the young man did housework and provided sexual services in exchange for gifts, guidance, protection and money from the senior man. This was a well-established if discreet custom, which lasted for decades. For the individual partners, it was likely to be temporary. In due course the younger man would move on; he might in turn acquire a 'mine wife' if he became a senior man in a compound. These relationships were not taken back to the homeland.

Back in the homeland, the rural homesteads had to keep functioning while many of their men were away at the mines. This too led to a significant adjustment, because the person left to run the homestead might well be a woman, such as the mineworker's wife. Now the older Mpondo men did not define manhood, *ubudoda*, in terms of warrior virtues, but in a very different way. As one ex-miner, Msana, put it:

> 'Ubudoda is to help people. If somebody's children don't have books or school fees or so, then you are going to help those children while the father cannot manage. Or if there is somebody who died, you go there and talk to people there. Or, if someone is poor – has no oxen – then you can take your own oxen and plow his fields. That is ubudoda, one who helps other people.' [Moodie writes:] I . . . asked whether there was not also a sort of manhood displayed by strength in fighting. Msana replied at once: 'No, that is not manhood. Such a person is called a killer.' (1994: 38)

Manhood, in this cultural setting, principally meant competent and benevolent management of a rural homestead, and participation in its community. Since a woman could perform these tasks, almost all the older Mpondo men logically held the view that a woman could have *ubudoda*. They were not denying that, in a patriarchal society, men ultimately have control. But they emphasized a conception of partnership between women and men in the building of homesteads, in which women could and often did perform masculine functions and thus participated in manhood.

But these gender arrangements, brought into existence by specific historical circumstances, were open to change. As the twentieth century wore on, the homestead agricultural economy declined. The apartheid government's policies of resettlement disrupted communities and created huge pools of displaced labour. The gold mining industry also changed. The workers became increasingly unionized, and the mine managements abandoned old forms of paternalism and sought new ways of negotiating with workers (though they continued to foment 'tribal' jealousies). In the 1970s, the old wage rates were abandoned and miners' incomes began to rise. This made it possible to support an urban household, or a non-agricultural household in the countryside, and broke the economic reciprocity between homestead and mine.

In these changed circumstances, the old migrant cultures were eroded, including their distinctive gender patterns. Younger Mpondo men no longer define 'manhood' in terms of presiding over a rural homestead. They simply equate it with the biological fact of maleness – which women cannot share. 'Thus', remarks Moodie, 'for the present generation of Mpondo, maleness and femaleness have been dichotomized again'. The women with manhood have disappeared from the scene.

Proletarianization has arrived at last, and with it a gender ideology closer to the European pattern. Among the younger mineworkers – more unionized, more militant and much better paid than their fathers – masculinity is increasingly associated with toughness, physical dominance and aggressiveness. This pattern of masculinity requires no reciprocity with women, who are, increasingly, left in the position of housewives dependent on a male wage earner.

There is much more in Moodie's complex and gripping work than can be summarized here: the labour process in the mines, life in the compounds, episodes of violence and resistance. As with Thorne's *Gender Play*, I am struck by the evidence of people's active creation of gender patterns. But the story of the mines gives a stronger impression of the constraints under which this creation is done, the impact of economic and political forces. There is a clearer view of the consequences of different gender strategies – prosperity and poverty, dominance and dependence. Above all, Moodie gives us a sense of the complex but powerful processes of historical change that transform gender arrangements over time.

Case 3. Bending gender

In the early 1980s, a new and devastating disease was identified, eventually named 'AIDS' (acquired immune deficiency syndrome). It was soon shown to be connected with a virus (human immunodeficiency virus: HIV) that killed people indirectly, by destroying their immune system's capacity to resist other diseases.

The global HIV/AIDS epidemic has produced a massive research response, ranging from the biological studies which discovered HIV, to social-science studies of the practices in which HIV is transmitted. The commonest form of 'behavioural' research, as it is usually called in health studies, is survey research using questionnaires. But research of that kind, though it yields useful statistics, gives limited understanding of the meanings that sexual encounters have for the partners, their place in the lives of the people involved.

It is precisely that kind of understanding that is crucial for AIDS prevention strategies – which, to be successful, must involve people in protecting themselves. Therefore, some researchers have turned to more sensitive and open-ended research strategies. One of the most notable products of this approach is Gary Dowsett's *Practicing Desire* (1996). This Australian study uses a traditional sociological method, the oral life-history, to create a vivid and moving portrait of homosexual sex in the era of AIDS.

Dowsett's study is based on interviews with twenty men. This may seem like a small number. But good life-history research is remarkably complex, produces a tremendous volume of evidence and many theoretical leads, and so cannot be hurried. Dowsett's study took nine years to get from first interviews to final publication. Each of the twenty respondents gave a narrative of his life, talked in intimate detail about relationships and sexual practices, discussed the communities he lived in, his jobs and workplaces, his relations with the wider world, and his connections with the HIV/AIDS epidemic. The evidence is remarkably rich, and raises important questions about gender. It is so rich, indeed, that I will discuss just one of the participants here.

Huey Brown, better known as Harriet, was in his late thirties at the time of the interviews. He is a well-known figure in the homosexual networks of an urban working-class community, 'Nullangardie', which has been proletarian (in Moodie's sense) for generations. His father was a truck driver, his mother a housewife. He left school at fourteen, and went to work at the checkout of a local supermarket. He has held a succession of unskilled jobs, mostly in cafes or hotels; he currently works as a sandwich maker. He doesn't have much money or education and has no professional certificate in anything. But Harriet is a formidable AIDS educator, not only organizing and fund-raising for AIDS-related events, but also being an informal teacher of safe sex and an influential community mentor.

Harriet became involved in homosexual sex in adolescence, not as a result of any identity crisis or alignment with a 'gay community' (which hardly existed in Nullangardie at the time), simply by engaging in informal and pleasurable erotic encounters with other boys and with men. Dowsett points out that homosexuality does not necessarily exist as a well-defined 'opposite' to heterosexuality. Among the boys and men of Nullangardie there are many sexual encounters and sexual networks which never get named, yet make an important part of sexuality as it really is.

Harriet is an enthusiast for sex, has had a very large number of partners, is skilful in many sexual techniques, adopts different positions in different sexual encounters, and gets diverse (and perverse) responses from different partners. As Dowsett remarks, this kind of evidence – by no means confined to Harriet's case – undermines any doctrine that there is a single, standard pattern of male sexuality.

Like many other people, Harriet wanted stable relationships, and has had three. The first was with a jealous man who beat him severely; the third was with a pre-op transsexual woman, which was hurtful in other ways. The second, with Jim, the love of Harriet's life, lasted nine years: 'It was a husband and wife team sort of thing. I looked after him and he looked after me.' Jim took the penetrative role in sex: 'He was that straight that he just didn't like a cock near his bum.' Jim worked in the building trade, they lived together, they baby-sat Jim's nieces and nephews, and some of Jim's family accepted the relationship quite well. Still, Harriet was no conventional wife. And, as Dowsett remarks, what are we to make of Jim?

> It sounds like an ordinary suburban life, except that his partner is a drag queen with breast implants and a penchant for insertive anal intercourse with casual partners on the odd occasion! ... Whatever Jim was or is, he certainly cannot be called 'gay', and when Harriet says: 'He [Jim] was that straight!' he means a sexually conventional male, not a heterosexually identified one. (1996: 94)

Yet after nine years Jim left Harriet – for a sixteen-year-old girl. There are gender practices here, but not gender boxes – the reality keeps escaping from the orthodox categories.

In some ways the most spectacular escape from the box was becoming a drag queen. In his late teens Huey began to hang out in a cross-dressing scene and became Harriet, working as a 'show girl'. In Australia, as in many other countries, there is a local tradition of drag entertainment involving mime, lip-synch singing, stand-up comedy and striptease. Harriet learnt the techniques of being a 'dragon', was good enough to pass as a woman on occasion, and even had operations to get breast implants. He acquired the camp style of humour and self-presentation which was part of the local tradition. Harriet now uses these techniques, and the local celebrity they gave him, for AIDS fundraising. But he notes a generational change. The younger men, more 'gay'-identified than 'camp', now like beefy male strippers better than the old-style drag shows.

Hotel work and drag shows do not pay well, and in a de-industrializing economy the economic prospects of unskilled workers are not good. In his late twenties, Harriet tried another form of work, prostitution. He worked in drag, and many of his customers presumed he was a woman. Some knew the score, or suspected, and for them his penis became part of the attraction. Harriet did some brothel work, but mostly worked independently on the street.

As Wendy Chapkis (1997) shows in a US/Dutch study, there are tremendous variations in the situations that sex workers face and in their level of control over the work. Harriet was right at one end of the spectrum, remaining firmly in control. He did not use narcotics, he offered only certain services, and he insisted on safe sex. He was skilful in sexual technique, and acquired loyal customers, some of whom stayed with him after he retired from the street – and after he took off the frocks. Even so, there was risk in street work, and a price to pay. Harriet learned to keep constantly aware of where the client's hands were. After several years and two arrests, he gave it up. Even so, his sexual reputation stayed with him, and on this account he was refused a job as an outreach worker with a local AIDS service organization.

Harriet's story (of which this is the barest outline) constantly calls into question the conventional categories of gender. It is not just that Harriet crosses gender boundaries. He certainly did that, with ingenuity and persistence, as a drag artist, surgical patient, wife, prostitute and activist. Yet Harriet is a man, not a transsexual male-becoming-female, and has mostly lived as a man. (In recognition of that, Dowsett writes, and I have followed his example, 'Harriet . . . he'.) The gender perplexity is also a question of Harriet's partners, customers and social milieu. Every element in the story seems to be surging beyond the familiar categories.

Dowsett argues that the ordinary categories of gender analysis are seriously inadequate to understand what is going on here. He mentions critiques of gender theory for being 'heterosexist', preoccupied with heterosexual relations and unable to understand people who are not heterosexual. Even when gender terms are used, in the context of homosexual sex they are transformed; an example is Harriet's comment on 'husband and wife'.

Sexual desire and practice thus seem to act like a powerful acid dissolving familiar categories:

> But Harriet also teaches us that these gender categories are subject to deconstruction in sex itself: some like being penetrated by a fully frocked transsexual; some clients eventually do not need the drag at all; pleasure and sensation, fantasy and fixation, are the currency in a sexual economy where the sexed and gendered bodies rather than determining the sexual engagement *desire* to lend themselves to even further disintegration. (Dowsett 1996: 117)

Dowsett thus ponders the limits of gender analysis, and questions the concept of gender identity. It is clear that gender is *present* in most of the episodes of Harriet's life. But it is also clear that gender does not *fix* Harriet's (or his partners') sexual practices. In his continuing research around the HIV/AIDS epidemic, Dowsett (2003) has argued forcefully that sexuality cannot be reduced to gender categories and must be understood in its own terms. Nevertheless, Harriet's story shows the constant *interplay* between gender and sexuality. Harriet's work as a prostitute rested on a gendered economy in Nullangardie which put money in the pockets of his clients – all of them men. Equally, their practice as clients rested on a masculine culture which regarded men as entitled to sexual gratification.

One of the lessons of this research is that we cannot treat gender relations as a mechanical system. Human action is creative, and we are always moving into historical spaces that no one has occupied before. At the same time, we do not create in a vacuum. We act in particular situations created by our own, and other people's, past actions. As shown by Harriet's sexual improvisations on materials provided by the gender order, we work on the past as we move into the future.

Case 4. Women, war and memory

One of the world's great experiments in gender equality was undertaken by the Soviet Union. The Bolshevik government established after the Russian revolutions of 1917, and the bitter civil war that followed, was formally committed to equal rights for women. At a time when, in much of the world, women were not even allowed to vote, a prominent feminist, Alexandra Kollontai, became minister for social welfare in the first Soviet government. The new regime made a major investment in girls' and women's education, women's health services and childcare facilities. Women's participation in industry and other forms of technical employment rose to levels never matched in the capitalist 'West'. The regime claimed to have achieved equality between women and men, and open access for women to all spheres of social and public life.

At the end of the 1980s, the system that held these ideals collapsed with stunning speed. In the countries that emerged from the former Soviet Union, different ideas about gender also emerged. Irina Novikova (2000: 119) notes how the attempt to create a new national identity for the post-Soviet regime in Latvia involved an appeal to surprisingly archaic models of gender: 'This started with a "return to the past", to the patri-archal traditions embedded in the paternalist and authoritarian model of the state that existed before Soviet annexation in 1939 . . . In this process, men were supposed to reorganize the state, while women/mothers were supposed to enshrine the "umbilical" role of a cultural gatekeeper within the family/home/nation/state.'

What happened in Latvia appears to have happened in most post-Soviet regimes. They are openly dominated by men, they marginalize women, and they weave together their nation-building with a hard, aggressive masculinity – exemplified by Vladimir Putin himself. It is, on the face of it, a stunning historical reversal, from a system of gender equality to a militant patriarchy. Why has this occurred?

Novikova, by profession a literary critic and historian, offers a fascin-ating answer in her essay 'Soviet and post-Soviet masculinities: after men's wars in women's memories'. This is an impressive example of the cultural analysis of gender, a research genre that raises questions not about individual lives, or particular institutional settings, but about the broad cultural meanings of gender and the way those meanings frame individual experience.

Novikova argues that the reassertion of local patriarchies was fuelled by the desire to reject the Soviet experiment as a whole:

It is commonly believed that men were emasculated, made effeminate, by the official Soviet model of sex equality. It is popularly believed that men's historic identity was lost, and now has to be restored. Thus the critical response to the failure of the whole Soviet utopian project is reflected in a gender dynamic. In the arguments of post-Soviet national-ist and conservative state rebuilding, the essential falseness of the utopian project is proved by the fact that it attributed feminine features to men and masculine features to women, thus reversing the 'natural' sex roles. (2000: 119)

This reaction is reinforced by the precarious position of the new regimes. The smaller ones are poor and dependent economies in a global capitalism dominated by the West, and even Russia suffered a terrible collapse of pride and strength at the end of the 1980s, from superpower to disaster area in a mere ten years. The celebration of a strong, competitive masculinity can be seen as a means of adjusting to this new, hostile and potentially overwhelming environment.

So far, the story seems straightforward; but it is more complicated than that. As Novikova also points out, the reassertion of masculine privilege could hardly have happened so quickly if the Soviet system had truly been as egalitarian as it claimed, if women had really been in a position of equal power with men.

Within ten years of the Bolshevik rising, its radicalism was in retreat and an authoritarian system was consolidating under Joseph Stalin. Stalin's regime was not just a violent dictatorship controlled by a group of ruthless men, it was a dictatorship that specialized in egalitarian lies. Under the progressive façade of 'communism' lived a system of inequality, not as spectacular as the inequalities of capitalism over in the United States, but certainly as deeply entrenched.

Part of this was a structure of gender inequality. Many of the gains women had made at the Revolution were rolled back in subsequent decades – for instance abortion rights. Women won a higher proportion of seats in Soviet parliaments than in almost any other part of the world – but the Soviet parliaments had no power. In the bodies that held real power (for instance the central executive of the communist party) women were a small minority. Women were present in the paid economy, certainly, but they also did a second shift – the unpaid housework and child care.

Yet, Novikova points out, women had an important symbolic place in Soviet culture, which derived from earlier periods of Russian history. This was a place as *mother*, especially as mother to sons. The regime put a lot of energy into reconciling the needs of women as workers with their role as mothers. But it also drew on powerful cultural themes about maternity. Indeed there was a level at which woman-as-mother was symbolically identified with Russia itself, sending forth sons-as-soldiers to liberate the world. A gendered myth of war was created which grew to full flower in the Second World War, and still existed when the regime tried to justify its disastrous military intervention in Afghanistan in the 1980s.

But women's actual experiences might be very different from the role in which women were cast by the regime. To explore this issue, Novikova turns to a little-discussed genre, women's war memoirs. She discusses the work of two writers. For lack of space I will skip over Elena Rzhevskaya, author of *Distant Rumble*, a Red Army intelligence officer personally involved in the search for Hitler, dead or alive, in Berlin in 1945. Here I will concentrate on the more recent writer, Svetlana Alexievich.

Alexievich is the author of *Zinc Boys*, a controversial book about the 'unknown war' the Soviet Union fought in Afghanistan. The title is an ironic allusion, on the one hand to the zinc coffins used by the Red Army in this war, on the other to the Soviet imagery of 'steel men', i.e. soldiers and workers in heroic narratives of earlier wars. The regime presented the Afghanistan war too as a crusade for peace and social justice. But it failed, despite superior technology and heavy casualties. Eventually the Soviet forces retreated from Afghanistan and the socialist government they supported – which was attempting reforms in women's position – collapsed. The victors were the militant misogynists of the Taliban movement; who were in turn overthrown by a US-led invasion; leading to the neo-colonial war being fought across Afghanistan and northern Pakistan now.

Alexievich interviewed veterans of the war in the 1980s, including women who had been there as military nurses. It is clear that the trauma created by this war was comparable to the failed American war in Vietnam, with similar levels of brutality, horror and doubt. Though the Soviet regime was more successful in suppressing public opposition, it merely drove the trauma underground. *Zinc Boys* opened the wounds again, to the anger both of veterans and of non-participants who wanted to have the whole ghastly mess forgotten.

Zinc Boys is an attempt at multiple autobiography, in which Alexievich as editor/author both uses and challenges the familiar cultural representation of the mother–son relationship in war. The writer's position is like that of the mother, but also unlike, especially confronting the emotional havoc among the Russian participants in this war. Instead of the welcoming and supportive national/maternal body, Alexievich and her readers confront body-memories of a different kind: male bodies, dead, torn apart, tortured, piled up and waiting for the zinc coffins – which happened to be in short supply.

The memories of defeat and mental devastation, and the powerful image of the war cemetery with unmarked graves, shatters the traditional imagery of the heroic male soldier at war. But the symbolic position of women in relation to this war is also untenable. The code of the strong woman, the amazon, the fighter for a larger cause, is destroyed by women's real memories of harassment, humiliation and being sexually exploited in the war zone by the men of their own side. Women's activism – i.e. participation in the crusade – simply made them vulnerable to exploitation, tearing up romantic dreams of marriage and love.

Returning from the war, women found this experience impossible to reconcile with the cultural expectations for womanhood, with the model of a virtuous worker-wife. The only way to handle the contradiction was to erase the memory. Hence some of the outrage created by Alexievich's text, which contested this erasure.

The men returning from the war turned in another direction. For them, the failed war had been an experience of collective impotency. After the American defeat in Vietnam, as a gripping study by Susan Jeffords (1989) has shown, American films and novels put a lot of energy into the reassertion of men's potency and authority vis-à-vis a more available target: local women, and the fiction of sex equality. Novikova shows the parallel in the late Soviet Union: 'Women are reminded that the masquerade is over, that equality was only a gift, and that female warriors are not to transgress the normal, biologically prescribed confines of their sex' (2000: 128).

Women's memoirs, Novikova argues, unveil the hidden gender dynamics behind the Soviet façade. This helps us to understand the post-Soviet shift away from the principle of gender equality. Especially this helps us to understand why it is often women themselves who support this shift. Having been through these traumas, they want 'only the right to forget their activism'. Many women become staunch proponents of the new patriarchy and the image of a powerful man.

Thus we can gain an understanding of the paradoxical gender patterns in post-Soviet life by a careful attention to cultural history, to the ways traditional gender images were both preserved and transformed in the Soviet era of apparent 'sex equality'.

Case 5. Change from below

Since gender research often reaches rather grim conclusions, it is nice to include a good news story. This one comes from a remote area of India. Some background is necessary.

The idea that men are (or should be) the producers or breadwinners, and women the consumers – though embedded in popular images of cave-men sallying out to hunt mammoths while women tend the fire in the home cave – is actually, historically speaking, very recent. In most hunter–gatherer societies, women collectively produce more food than men do. In peasant societies, women are a vital, regular part of the agricultural labour force, working together with men in the fields or raising their own specialized crops. In many African societies, women have been prominent as traders.

Under colonialism, however, these arrangements were disrupted, for instance by the use of indigenous men for mining or plantation labour and women as household servants. In late nineteenth- and twentieth-century colonialism, and in the era of globalization that followed, a breadwinner/housewife model, created in the industrial cities of the North Atlantic world, spread around the world as a popular ideal of modern gender relations (however unrealistic it often was). The economic development and modernization programmes that were set up across the 'underdeveloped' world in the 1950s and 1960s by newly independent governments, by Western aid agencies and by the United Nations typically assumed the breadwinner/housewife model and directed almost all of their resources to men.

The massive injustices that resulted came under fire from feminists in the 1970s, both in recipient countries and in aid agencies. A 'Women in Development' movement emerged, arguing that resources should be re-directed equitably to women. And gradually this principle has been taken up by aid agencies. But how could it be done, in post-colonial societies where men continued to control state agencies, local governments, banks, and trading and manufacturing corporations, not to mention land? One of the solutions evolved was 'micro-credit' schemes. In these, women – either individually or in cooperatives – can access small amounts of credit to expand their existing production activities, or to start new small businesses, in the hope that they would soon be self-supporting. The most famous of these schemes is the Grameen Bank in Bangladesh, whose founder, Muhammad Yunus, was awarded the Nobel Peace Prize in 2006.

But this approach isn't trouble-free. In places where men have strong patriarchal power, resources ear-marked for women may simply be appropriated by men; where the resources do get into women's hands, the new situation may be strongly resented by men; micro-credit schemes sometimes have the unwelcome side-effect of triggering domestic violence. Reform in the economic position of women therefore seemed to require programmes involving men, to achieve change in the local gender order. Accordingly, a more comprehensive 'Gender and Development' strategy was proposed, to include men and gender relations in the process. This was immediately controversial among feminists, who saw the prospect of men taking over gender policy, and the small stream of resources now directed to women being drained back towards men (White 2000).

Nevertheless, a good many initiatives involving men in gender change have recently been taken, in many countries. Vivid accounts have been published in a book edited by the Indian sociologist Radhika Chopra (2007), herself a specialist in gender and family studies. The authors tell about struggles to support sex workers' rights, girls' education, the mothers of the disappeared, gay rights, and against the killing of female foetuses. One of the chapters, called 'Enterprising women, supportive men: micro credit networks in the north-east', discusses how the economic strategy works at face-to-face level.

The author, a young social scientist called Subhashim Goswami, tells the story of a trek into the hills in the Meghalaya region, in company with a fieldworker for a development NGO (non-profit, non-government organization) active in north-eastern India. Goswami had heard about this fieldworker, Prince Thangkhiew, during research in the neighbouring province of Assam. They eventually met in a country town – with some difficulty, because Prince was almost always out in the villages. Goswami started the usual research procedure, sitting down for an interview; but after a while Prince said: 'I can't tell you about my work sitting across a table like this, you'll have to come to the villages with me and see for yourself; if you have to, walk long hours, maybe on mud paths, eat what they give you, sleep on the floor' (Goswami 2007: 140). So they did, leaving the same day, travelling on foot and on crowded local buses, from village to village, through the 'breathtakingly beautiful', but extremely impoverished, hill country of the Khasi people.

Prince worked officially as an intermediary between the NGO and the self-help groups to which it gave small grants. These grants allowed local people to set up diverse income-generating businesses, ranging through grocery shops, vegetable and rice marketing, school supplies, raising pigs, and broomstick cultivation. The idea was to create self-sustaining local sources of income, without burdening poor people with interest payments on loans.

Prince, however, did a great deal more than administer funds. He was a skilful and committed community organizer, who had spent five years getting to know the local people and intended to live permanently among them. He was, by Goswami's account, a driven man who was pursuing, with astonishing energy, a vision of poverty eradication from below. And the majority of the people he worked with in this programme were women. Indeed, 'It would not be an exaggeration to state that the support base that Prince had created in the East-Khasi Hills has been women-centric and women oriented' (Goswami 2007: 156).

Khasi society is matrilineal; inheritance of property mainly flows through the youngest daughter. This does not mean a society ruled by women; older men generally control the village councils or *dorbars*, so Prince constantly negotiates with men as well. But it does mean that women are fully involved with production, have a role in decision-making, and are therefore able to set up self-help economic units.

Prince helps with the technical steps involved – such as organizing the signing of contracts for grants – but also stays in touch afterwards, helping with networking and strategies, resolving conflicts and passing on skills. Prince obviously has respect and rapport with local women, a strong 'joking relationship' as Goswami puts it, knowing a great many by name, chatting freely with groups of women in kitchens, on buses and in the markets as he moves around the region. Prince also has great rapport with local children, cares about their health and education, and sees the children, indeed, as the long-term answer to the problem of mass poverty.

This NGO's work is not formally intended as a gender reform programme, as far as I can tell – its intentions are community development and poverty reduction. But to a striking degree it involves working across the gender boundary that is conventional in most parts of India, creating a cross-gender alliance that empowers women. Doing so has required sustained effort on Prince's part as well as trust and adventurousness on the part of local women. And perhaps, also, the story implies a level of acceptance and cooperation by local men that is worth celebrating.

Other notable studies might have been included in this chapter; more will be mentioned through the book. I hope these five are enough to show the diversity of gender dynamics, their complexity and their power. In talking about gender, we are not talking about simple differences or fixed categories. We are talking about relationships, boundaries, practices, identities and images that are actively created in social processes. They come into existence in particular historical circumstances, shape the lives of people in profound and often contradictory ways, and are subject to historical struggle and change. How the intellectuals of the world have tried to understand these processes will be the subject of the next chapter.

3

Gender theorists and gender theory

In the majority world, 1: Raden Ajeng Kartini

A little over a hundred years ago in Java, then part of the Dutch East Indies, a young woman in a ruling-class Muslim family decided to be a writer and teacher, and advertised for a pen-friend in the Netherlands. The young woman's name was Kartini and the pen-friend she found was Stella Zeehandelaar, a social democrat who helped to put her in touch with European progressive thought. Kartini and her two sisters were developing an agenda for reforming Javanese society and culture, especially the position of women. Kartini was vigorously opposed to the institution of polygamy, and critical of the seclusion of women and their lack of education. Therefore she proposed to remain unmarried herself, to launch a programme of action. She planned to set up a school for the daughters of the elite, on the idea that the aristocracy should provide a model for change; and she began publishing essays.

These activities by a woman, however, were thought damaging to the honour of her family. Though her father had provided a private education for Kartini, he would not send her to train as a teacher in Holland. Nor could she get government support for the planned school. Eventually the family, following custom, arranged a good marriage for her, and she bowed to pressure. It killed her: she died from complications of her first childbirth, aged twenty-four.

Kartini's letters to Stella, in which this story of hope and disappointment are told, were collected after her death, censored, and published in 1911, a little later translated into English under the sentimental title

Letters of a Javanese Princess. (For the tougher uncensored version, see Kartini 2005.) They became a classic of Dutch and colonial literature, and Raden Ajeng Kartini became a heroine of the Indonesian independence movement. I have never seen her work referred to in the English-language literature on gender, except for regional studies specifically about Indonesia.

Kartini was not trying to develop a 'theory of gender' – not many people at the time were. Yet her writing deals directly with a number of the questions that a theory of gender must address: the institution of the family, gender divisions of labour, ideologies of womanhood, and strategies of change in gender relations. And she does this in the context of colonial society, criticizing racism, and problematizing the relationship between global centre and periphery that is now a crucial issue in feminist thought.

To speak of theories of gender abstractly is to imply that all the theories have the same object of knowledge. This can be, at best, only approximately correct. Ideas are created in varying circumstances, by people with different backgrounds and different training. History throws different problems at them. It is not surprising that they formulate their intellectual projects, and understand their object of knowledge, in differing ways.

This sociology-of-knowledge principle was first applied to gender theories by Viola Klein in a now-forgotten classic, *The Feminine Character: History of an Ideology* (1946). In a later generation it was re-emphasized by feminist 'standpoint epistemology'. To understand theories of gender, then, it is necessary to consider the intellectuals who produced them and the situations they faced. I will try to do this historically. My main focus will be on the global metropole, since that is where today's dominant modes of thinking arose; but I will bear in mind the geopolitics of knowledge. I assume, as Kartini and Stella did, that the attempt at communication across different regions and situations is worthwhile.

In the metropole, 1: from Christine de Pizan to Simone de Beauvoir

The gender theories of the global metropole are products of a secular, rationalist and sceptical culture which took its modern shape, so far as the human sciences are concerned, in the second half of the nineteenth century. The gender theories that began to emerge then resulted from the gradual transformation of older discourses that were religious and moralistic, dating from times before modern imperialism.

Mediaeval Christianity inherited, from the saints and sages of the ancient Mediterranean world, a tradition of misogyny that to a modern reader is startling in its viciousness. The writings of Christian intellectuals are peppered with declarations of the inferiority of women in mind and body, and the danger they represent if men succumb to their wiles (Blamires 1992). There was, nevertheless, a counter-tradition defending women. In 1405 this was brought together in a great allegory, *The Book of the City of Ladies*, by Christine de Pizan in France. Christine refuted, point by point, the traditional abuse of women, building an allegorical 'city' in her text which would be a safe space for women. She made a claim, not to social or economic equality, but to equality of respect.

The tradition of the moral defence of womanhood continued through the Reformation and the early stages of imperialism, especially among groups like the Quakers who defended women's equal right to preach, i.e. to exercise religious authority. It was still available at the time of the French Revolution, and was drawn on by Mary Wollstonecraft's *Vindication of the Rights of Woman* (1792), produced in immediate response to the declaration of the 'Rights of Man'. The early suffrage movement in the United States was in large part a religious movement. The Seneca Falls convention in 1848, often seen as the moment when modern feminism appeared, borrowed the moralizing language of the Declaration of Independence for its message.

Already, however, religion was being displaced by science as the major frame of intellectual life. Nineteenth-century science was actively concerned with problems related to gender. Charles Darwin, the towering figure in evolutionary thought, in *The Origin of Species* (1859) made inheritance and biological selection into first-rank intellectual issues. Darwin's later work specifically addressed the choice of sexual partners and the evolutionary role of sex as a form of reproduction. This occurred at a moment when the gender division of labour, and symbolic divisions between women and men, were at an extreme. It is not surprising that in this milieu evolutionary thought – 'Darwinism' more than Darwin – produced the idea of a biological basis for all forms of social difference, including the racial hierarchies then being constructed by the expanding empires, and including gender division in the metropole.

Gender issues ran through early attempts by male intellectuals to formulate a science of society and a theory of social progress. The French philosopher Auguste Comte, the founder of positivism and a figure almost as influential as Darwin, gave close attention to the social function of women in the first-ever 'treatise of sociology', *System of Positive Polity* (1851). Women were, in his view, an important base for the coming utopian society – but only if they remained in their proper sphere as comforters and nurturers of men. His most distinguished follower, the

British philosopher John Stuart Mill, took a more radical view in the famous essay *The Subjection of Women* (1869), arguing the case for equality, and seeing the basic reason for inequality not in men's moral superiority but in physical force. When Lester Ward wrote the first major theoretical statement in American sociology, *Dynamic Sociology* (1883), he offered a long analysis of the 'reproductive forces' with a detailed critique of 'sexuo-social inequalities' such as unequal education for girls and boys. In 1879 the German labour leader August Bebel published a book, *Woman and Socialism*, which became a best-seller. Marx's colleague Friedrich Engels wrote a long essay, *The Origin of the Family, Private Property and the State* (1884), which drew on academic debates about the history of the family and the idea of 'matriarchy', as well as socialists' concerns about 'the woman question' as an issue of social reform.

Why did the men do this? Basically, because the woman question had been placed on the agenda by an emerging movement of women, which was strong in exactly those social groups from which the new social scientists came. The emancipation of women became a test of the 'progress' achieved by any society.

Women intellectuals in these generations were operating under such difficulties that they were unlikely to produce theoretical treatises themselves. (Among other things, women were then excluded from almost all universities.) One hardly finds a 'theory of gender' in the writings of feminist intellectuals like Harriet Martineau in Britain, Susan B. Anthony in the United States, or Maybanke Wolstenholme in Australia – though one finds many insights into the mechanisms of patriarchy. Their attention was more focused on the critique of prejudice among men, or on practical problems of organizing for the suffrage, law reform, and education for women.

When more theoretical writing by women developed, in texts such as Olive Schreiner's *Woman and Labour* (1911), it was closely connected with economic issues. Schreiner analysed the 'parasitism' of bourgeois women and the refusal of bourgeois society to recognize its exploitation of working women. At the same time, women in the labour movement asked how far working-class and bourgeois women had shared interests. Alexandra Kollontai's *The Social Basis of the Woman Question* (1909) argued vehemently that there was no general 'women's question', and that support by working-class women for socialism was the only path towards true equality. This did not prevent Kollontai arguing for separate organization of women within the labour movement, and opening debates about sexual freedom and the reform of marriage.

The intellectuals of Paris, London, St Petersburg and New York were living in the heartlands of the greatest wave of imperial expansion the world has ever known. Explorers, conquerors, missionaries and curious travellers gathered an immense fund of information about gender arrangements in the non-European world, which they often thought were survivals from the primitive days of mankind. Texts such as Engels' *Origin* testify to the fascination of this information for metropolitan intellectuals. Early social anthropology is full of it. Popular imperialism put many exotic images of gender into circulation: polygamy, marriage by conquest, concubinage, amazon women, primitive promiscuity. A serious comparative science of gender was slow to emerge; but in the late nineteenth and early twentieth century the news from the empire was already acting alongside feminism to destabilize belief in a fixed gender order. Already gender debates were dealing with a range of issues that we can recognize in modern gender research: power ('subjection'), sexuality ('phylogenetic forces', 'free love') and the division of labour ('parasitism').

Yet the way they were interpreted was very different from approaches a hundred years later. To the bourgeois and socialist intelligentsia alike, men and women were absolute categories and the main determinant of gender patterns was the dynamic of progress, whether gradual or revolutionary. From Mill to Schreiner it was progress – moral, economic and political – that was thought to be breaking the bonds of ancient custom and lifting gender relations onto a higher and more rational plane. The idea of a 'theory of gender' as an intellectual undertaking in its own right was alien to this way of thought. But such an idea was soon to come.

A crucial step towards it was taken by the newly created depth psychology. When the Viennese nerve specialist Sigmund Freud became convinced that many of his patients' troubles were psychological, not physical, in origin, he explored their emotional lives for causes, and developed new interpretive methods to do so. His patients' talk, during long courses of therapy, gave him masses of evidence about the troubled emotional interior of the bourgeois family. This was documented in stunning case histories, the most famous being 'Dora' (1905) and the 'Wolf Man' (1918). They underpinned theoretical texts in which Freud expounded the concepts of unconscious motivation (*The Interpretation of Dreams*, 1900), childhood sexuality, the oedipus complex and the transformations of desire and attachment in the course of growing up (*Three Essays on the Theory of Sexuality*, 1905), and the connections between depth psychology and culture (*Civilization and its Discontents*, 1930).

By the 1920s Freud's ideas had spread far beyond their first technical audience and had become a cultural force. It was clear that, whether right or wrong in detail, Freud had put his finger on problems which were both troubling and important for modern Western societies. Freud was not directly a supporter of the women's movement, but doubtless was influenced by contemporary feminism in the problems he addressed. His first major follower, Alfred Adler, had close links to the social-democratic labour movement, and did explicitly support feminism. Adler (1927) made the critique of masculinity a centrepiece of his revision of psychoanalysis. These pioneers, and the next generation of psycho-analysts who debated sexuality, femininity and masculinity in the 1920s and early 1930s, showed that the gender divisions of adulthood were not fixed from the start of life. Rather, the adult patterns were con-structed in a conflict-ridden process of development over the life-course. This was a decisive shift in ideas about gender. Nineteenth-century thought, even feminism, had taken the fixed characters of men and women more or less for granted.

The next step, to a fully social theory of gender, followed quickly. The landmark was Mathilde Vaerting's *The Dominant Sex*, first pub-lished in 1921. Vaerting, a reforming educator, was one of the first two women ever appointed at professorial level in a German university. She met with an extremely hostile reaction, was thrown out of her job when Hitler came to power, and never held a university chair again. Under-standably, she had a lifelong interest in the sociology of power.

The Dominant Sex criticized the notion of a fixed masculine and feminine character on sociological grounds. Basing herself shakily on a speculative history of ancient Egypt and Sparta, and more firmly on an environmental view of character, Vaerting argued that masculinity and femininity basically reflected power relations. In societies where women held power, men showed the very characteristics which bourgeois society saw as quintessentially feminine. In developing this argument, Vaerting created the first extended inter-disciplinary theory of gender. Her argu-ment linked psychological patterns with social structure, and distin-guished law, the division of labour, and ideology as spheres of gender domination. She even offered an amazing prediction of Men's Liberation as a sequel of feminism. Her work was rapidly translated into English, and was a focus of controversy in the 1920s; but in the European up-heavals that followed, her work faded into obscurity.

A better empirical base for gender theory was taking shape about the same time in social anthropology, with its newly developed technique of field study, 'ethnography'. The best-known ethnographers, from the Polish Bronislaw Malinowski to the American Margaret Mead, paid close attention to sex and gender. Malinowski used ethnographic infor-mation in a famous critique of psychoanalysis, arguing that the 'oedipus complex' as described by Freud was not universal. Mead's early research in Samoa reinforced the idea of cultural diversity in sexual conduct. Then, in a widely read book called *Sex and Temperament in Three Primi-*

tive Societies (1935), based on fieldwork in New Guinea, Mead – like Vaerting – rejected the idea of a fixed relationship between biological sex and gendered character. Ethnographers profoundly relativized the picture of gender. They gave credible and often sympathetic portraits of non-Western societies where gender arrangements functioned perfectly well, though along quite different lines from bourgeois life in the metropole.

Awareness of the relativity of gender helped to popularize the concept of 'sex roles' in the 1940s and 1950s. This was a simple application of the general notion that people's social conduct reflects conformity to cultural norms for the social positions they occupy. The most influential formulation was made by the most influential sociological theorist of the era, the Harvard University professor Talcott Parsons (Parsons and Bales 1956). Parsons's much-quoted characterization of the male role as 'instrumental' and the female role as 'expressive' defined a difference of social function. Other writers about sex roles simply parked the instrumental/expressive distinction on top of biological difference, and presumed that the role norms corresponded to the natural difference. But Parsons treated the whole gender process as a consequence of a social system's need for integration and stability.

The popularity of what amounted to a theory of social conformity in the repressive 1950s is not surprising. Yet sex role theory was concerned also with *changes* in sex roles, notable in wartime. Mirra Komarovsky (who many years later became president of the American Sociological Association, the second woman ever elected to that position) had good reason to theorize 'Cultural contradictions and sex roles', the title of a 1946 paper. Sex role change was also possible for men. Helen Hacker suggested this in a pioneering paper, 'The new burdens of masculinity' (1957). In consumer capitalism and suburban life, she argued, expressive functions were being added to instrumental, so that men were now expected to show interpersonal skills as well as being 'sturdy oaks'.

There was a feminist colouring in some sex role discussions, including Hacker's. But the renewal of feminist gender theory in the mid-century was basically the work of Simone de Beauvoir in France. *The Second Sex* (1949), the most famous of all modern feminist texts, drew on psychoanalysis, literature and the activist philosophy worked out by de Beauvoir's partner Jean-Paul Sartre, to challenge gender categories and gender domination at the same time. Refusing to take the polarity of masculine and feminine for granted, de Beauvoir explored how women were constituted as 'other' in the consciousness of men. She went on, in a remarkable series of social portraits, to explore the variety of ways in which women could respond to this situation and constitute themselves – not escaping from gender, for that was impossible, but realizing gender differently in different life projects. This work, too, was stimulated by the upheaval of war, and de Beauvoir's topics overlapped substantially with those of sex role research. But what she could see in these topics was different, because her approach stemmed from a political critique of the subordination of women.

By the mid-century this was exceptional. Psychoanalysis had mostly become a socially conservative branch of medicine, much more concerned to normalize people than to pursue an agenda of liberation. Sex role theory was also, in the main, a conservative approach – especially as it was applied in counselling, social work and schools. Simone de Beauvoir's cutting edge found many admirers, but no immediate popular response.

In the metropole, 2: from Women's Liberation to queer theory

It was this cultural situation in the mid-century, as well as the energy from young women in the radical social movements of the 1960s, that gave an explosive quality to the Women's Liberation movement. An extraordinarily rapid mobilization occurred in the late 1960s and early 1970s, across much of the advanced capitalist world. This movement produced a categorical approach to gender, emphasizing the solidarity of women as an oppressed group or a 'sex class' – which ran counter to the deconstructive trend of earlier gender theory. US feminism especially was sweepingly hostile to psychoanalysis.

The characteristic Women's Liberation view was based on a categorical theory of power. The term 'patriarchy' was fished up from an anthropological backwater and used to name systems of male power and oppression of women. Patriarchy had to be confronted by an autonomous women's movement, and the demand for the liberation of women was a revolutionary demand. This view was expounded in a torrent of pamphlets and a series of vivid books, from Sheila Rowbotham's *Women's Liberation and the New Politics* (1969) to Robin Morgan's famous anthology *Sisterhood is Powerful* (1970) and Shulamith Firestone's *Dialectic of Sex* (1971). Even men influenced by the new feminism began to speak this language. Calls for 'male liberation', in solidarity with women's liberation rather than against it, soon appeared (Sawyer 1970).

The radical movements of the time in the USA, influenced by the Civil Rights struggle and the struggle against the neo-colonial war in Vietnam, shared a belief that all systems of oppression could and would be overthrown. This perspective was immediately shared by the first theorists of Gay Liberation, who added sexual oppression to the agenda, in street politics and in texts such as Dennis Altman's *Homosexual: Oppression and Liberation* (1972) and Guy Hocquenghem's *Homosexual Desire* (1972).

By the later 1970s, however, a gender-specific view had come to prominence in the United States and Britain. This view sharply separated gender struggles from others, or saw the oppression of women as the root of all social inequality. This perspective was dramatically presented by the US theologian Mary Daly in *Gyn/Ecology* (1978). Daly tried to create a new conceptual and symbolic language to express women's consciousness and women's anger against men, as part of an effort to create a distinct women's culture. The social radicalism of early Women's Liberation was defined as an impure variant of feminism.

The impulse of Women's Liberation was so powerful, however, that it launched a whole spectrum of theories. A categorical theory that focused on the division of labour, emphasizing the economic exploitation of women within the family, was proposed in a famous essay 'The main enemy' by Christine Delphy (1970) in France. Debate ran through the 1970s on how to theorize women's domestic labour, and whether capitalists or husbands were the main beneficiaries of women's work (Malos 1980).

The familiar 'sex role' concept was radicalized. This was now treated as an account of the social controls that hampered women. In the United States there was a wave of enthusiasm for the attempt by the psychologist Sandra Bem (1974) to define and measure 'androgyny' as a goal of sex role reform. A debate about the 'male sex role' and how men could break out of it, or at least bend it, began in the United States and spilled into several other countries (Pleck and Sawyer 1974).

Other feminists used the techniques of structuralism, the most influential intellectual movement in the human sciences at the time. In a long essay called 'The traffic in women: notes on the "political economy" of sex', Gayle Rubin (1975) integrated feminism and anthropology in a sophisticated model of 'the sex/gender system'. This was perhaps the most ambitious theory of gender since Vaerting's. It was not isolated. A structural account of women's subordination had been proposed as early as 1966 by Juliet Mitchell in an essay 'Women: the longest revolution'. In 1974, in *Psychoanalysis and Feminism*, Mitchell proposed a complex theory of the reproduction of class society and patriarchy over time.

Mitchell's book, along with the work of Nancy Chodorow (1978) in the United States, marked a striking reversal of the feminist coolness towards psychoanalysis in the English-speaking world. The power of Freudian concepts to explain people's acceptance of oppressive social relations was again recognized. In France the rejection of psychoanalysis had not been so marked, and, in the wake of Women's Liberation, adaptations of Lacan's version of psychoanalysis were undertaken by a number of women. A key goal was to find a level of human reality which escaped the phallocentric structure of ordinary language and consciousness. Julia Kristeva's *Revolution in Poetic Language* (1974) and Luce Irigaray's essay *This Sex Which is Not One* (1977) were perhaps the most influential.

A simpler feminist adaptation of psychoanalysis and developmental psychology, Carol Gilligan's *In a Different Voice* (1982), captured popular attention in the English-speaking world and became a best-seller. This was a return to categorical theory at the level of 'voice'. It was widely read as proving that men and women had different moral senses, and fed into the acceptance of a milder version of feminism as a kind of organizational reform in the state and the corporate world.

By the late 1970s, the new feminism in the rich countries had established a strong cultural presence and was establishing an organizational presence in government and in universities. It won resources to run programmes such as shelters for battered women, women's health centres, equal employment opportunity programmes, and school initiatives for girls. These programmes rapidly took hold where there were labour or social-democratic governments, in Scandinavia, Canada, Australia and (at regional level) Germany. This created sharp debate, given the Women's Liberation view of the state as part of the patriarchal system. The work of feminist bureaucrats posed new intellectual questions: how to understand the organizations in which they found themselves, as well as how to understand the policy problems which the programmes addressed.

Accordingly, new branches of theory and research developed. A number of theorists reconsidered the state, increasingly seen as a gendered institution of great complexity, with possibilities of internal change (see chapter 7). Research institutes and monitoring programmes were set up, such as the Norwegian Likestillingssenteret (Centre for Gender Equality). A whole genre of feminist or feminist-inspired policy studies began to appear. To take just one field, education: notable policy studies range from the pioneering Australian report *Girls, School and Society* (1975), sponsored by the national Schools Commission, to the very sophisticated British study *Closing the Gender Gap* by Madeleine Arnot and her colleagues (1999).

In metropolitan universities, the 1970s and 1980s saw a huge growth of feminist or feminist-inspired research in almost every discipline of the humanities and social sciences, and to a lesser extent in the natural sciences. In sociology, for instance, sex and gender – formerly a marginal field of low prestige – became the most active field of research in the whole discipline. Feminist historiography had become a large enterprise, fuelled by the need to correct the massive biases of patriarchal history, and the recognition of gender as an important category of historical knowledge (Scott 1986). Feminist science studies flourished, casting new light on an area that once was thought a perfect proof of male superiority (Harding 1986).

Journals which published research about sex roles, gender, women and, eventually, men multiplied. Some became high-prestige academic journals – notably *Signs*, a US feminist journal launched in 1975. In the 1990s and 2000s women's studies mutated into 'gender studies' embracing lesbian, gay and transgender issues, amid controversy as to whether this would destroy its political edge, and continues to develop. In the 2000s, for instance, the Swedish government established a number of new gender studies chairs, and funded an inter-university 'Centre of Gender Excellence' programme to stimulate research.

At one level, all this was a startling success for feminism. The patriarchal monologue in universities was interrupted almost at once, and a new social base for feminist thought was established. Yet Women's Liberation movement activists looked on the early stages of this triumph with distrust, fearing that academic feminism would lose its political urgency, separate itself from grassroots campaigns, and become unintelligible to working-class women.

Everything that the activists feared has come to pass. A large part of gender theory in the English-speaking metropole has become abstract, contemplative or analytical in style, or focuses entirely on cultural subversions. A measure of the shift is this: when three English feminists wrote a survey of conceptual literature called *Theorizing Gender* (Alsop, Fitzsimons and Lennon 2002), their book made practically no reference to girls' education, domestic violence, women's health, gender mainstreaming, economic development or any other *policy* question that feminists had been grappling with – and did not have a single entry for the 'state' in the index. The kind of theory they were writing about had ceased to connect with such problems. But it dealt at great length with sexuality, personal identity, symbolism and difference.

The main points of reference for this kind of theorizing were intellectual developments among philosophers who worked on problems other than gender, notably Michel Foucault and Jacques Derrida in France. The feminist application of Foucault's studies of discourse, subjectification, micro-politics and the regulation of bodies has been widespread. Derrida's influence has been more indirect, though possibly more profound. His argument on the indefinite deferral of meaning in language, and his technique of deconstruction, have been taken as warrant for questioning the stability of all concepts and all identities – including the categories on which feminist thought rested.

A book by a young US philosopher pursuing this theme, Judith Butler's *Gender Trouble* (1990), became by far the most influential text in academic feminism in the 1990s, was read beyond the academic world and is still the subject of extended debate (Lloyd 2007). Butler argued that there are no fixed foundations of gender categories and therefore of feminist strategy. Gender is performative, bringing identities into existence through action, rather than being the expression of some pre-existing reality. In Butler's treatment, gender radicalism consists not of mobilization around an identity (such as 'women'), but of actions that subvert identity, disrupt gender dichotomy and displace gender norms.

This book's enormous popularity in the metropole was not only due to post-structuralist fashion. It fed into a new kind of politics. By the 1980s the new left had fragmented, and Women's Liberation as a coherent movement was gone – split over issues of sexuality, race, and relations with the state. Externally, feminism was running into stiffer resistance. A strong religious-right mobilization campaigned against abortion rights and sexual freedoms. A broader political reaction stopped the Equal Rights Amendment in the United States, and brought the Reagan, Thatcher and Kohl administrations to power. In countries where centre-left governments were elected in the 1980s, including France and Australia, early openings towards feminism were squeezed by the rising influence of neoliberal market ideology.

There continued to be gains for gender reform, most spectacularly in Scandinavia, where women arrived en masse in party politics. In 1991, for instance, the leaders of all three major parties in Norway were women, including the prime minister, Gro Harlem Brundtland. But open homophobia re-emerged in mainstream politics, particularly vicious around the HIV/AIDS epidemic. In the most powerful states, a political oscillation in the 1990s and 2000s between centrist governments, hard neoliberalism and aggressive nationalism has meant limited space even for a mild official feminism, though that has continued to exist in the machinery of the United Nations (UN) and the European Union (EU).

This course of events provoked many re-examinations of feminism and gender theory. One move was led by Black feminists in North America, who argued that uncritical use of the category 'women' in feminism concealed the realities of racism. For some American Black feminists, including bell hooks (1984), that argument led back to the inclusive radicalism of early Women's Liberation and a renewed concern with integrating class, race and gender struggles. But the main effect was a growth of identity politics within feminism and a kind of standpoint theory, illustrated in Patricia Hill Collins' *Black Feminist Thought* (1991). This produced multiple positions representing the outlook of particular groups of women, especially those who were marginalized within the society of the metropole: Black feminism, Latina feminism and lesbian feminism. New literatures emerged, even in the rich countries, of research and testimony from cultural backgrounds beyond the establishment. Lourdes Torres (1991), for instance, notes the growth of Latina writing in the United States, especially a new genre of autobiography. Some difficult re-thinking began. White feminists had mainly seen the family as a site of women's oppression – much as Kartini had. But in a context of metropolitan racism, the family (especially the extended family) might be a crucial asset for Black women, and for women in recent immigrant communities.

The most widely influential body of theory, however, was work that re-examined the founding categories of feminism as such. Feminist sociologists, in the United States particularly, explored the micro-foundations of the gender order, looking closely at the way gender categorization was achieved in everyday interaction. A paper called 'Doing Gender' (West and Zimmerman 1987) crystallized this approach and had a wide influence. Feminist philosophers re-considered the relationship of the body to gender categories. Some of them returned to an emphasis on the unbridgeable difference between women's and men's bodies, seeing gender always as embodied experience in which the supposed gap between 'sex' and 'gender' is reduced to nothing (Grosz 1994).

Particularly influential was cultural and philosophical writing that emphasized the fragility of all identity categories, and saw gender as, in principle, fluid rather than fixed. A new wave in lesbian and gay thought, which came to be known as queer theory, took this for granted and criticized the cultural constraints, summed up in the word 'heteronormativity', that pushed people into fixed identities within gender binaries. This was energized by new forms of political and cultural activism, especially from a younger generation, that defied conventional categories, played radical games with gender meanings, and set about 'queering' everything in sight – troubling older forms of lesbian and gay activism as well (for a wry and perceptive account see Reynolds 2002). Butler's *Gender Trouble* became an icon for this whole cultural movement.

More bread-and-butter research continued, particularly in the social sciences, which pushed beyond the beginnings made by women's studies. A feminist organization theory emerged, as sociologists such as Joan Acker in the United States and Peta Tancred in Canada analysed the gender regimes of bureaucracies and corporations (Mills and Tancred 1992). The exhaustion of sex role theory had left the discussion of 'Men's Liberation' stranded. New beginnings of research on masculinity were made in the mid-1980s, linking gay theory and feminist gender analysis. In the 1990s, research on the social construction of masculinity multiplied in the rich countries, and a theorization of multiple masculinities and the relations among them emerged (Connell 1995). Research on masculinities rapidly internationalized and is now found in all parts of the world.

At much the same time, the difficulty of understanding gender on a world scale began to concern theorists in the metropole. Women's Liberation had produced a theory of patriarchy which, in its more sophisticated forms, had historical depth and worldwide reach (Reiter 1977). Later texts such as Maria Mies' *Patriarchy and Accumulation on a World Scale* (1986) and Spike Peterson's *Critical Rewriting of Global Political Economy* (2003) turned the focus on colonialism and world capitalism as gendered systems, where gender was dynamic not static. Feminist analyses of international relations, such as Cynthia Enloe's *Bananas, Beaches and Bases* (1990), showed the gender dimension in relations between states and in international trade. The interplay of gender relations, ethnicity and modern nationalisms emerged as an important theme in Nira Yuval-Davis' *Gender and Nation* (1997). This work has had a growing impact as 'globalization' has become a central issue in politics and popular consciousness.

In the majority world, 2: from the Decade for Women on

During the 1980s, partly as a result of the UN Decade for Women, 1975–85, metropolitan feminists' interest in women and feminism in other parts of the world rose sharply. Conferences multiplied, book series appeared, and Robin Morgan, editor of the classic US Women's Liberation anthology *Sisterhood is Powerful*, edited a sequel, *Sisterhood is Global* (1984).

Some years later Chandra Talpade Mohanty, a diasporic Indian intellectual working in the United States, published a brilliant critique of this literature in an essay 'Under Western eyes'. Its main tendency, she argued, was to homogenize 'third world women' into a single category of victimhood, representing the extremity of gender oppression:

> This average third world woman leads an essentially truncated life based on her feminine gender (read: sexually constrained) and her being 'third world' (read: ignorant, poor, uneducated, tradition-bound, domestic, family-oriented, victimized, etc.) . . . in contrast to the (implicit) self-representation of Western women as educated, as modern, as having control over their own bodies and sexualities, and the freedom to make their own decisions. (Mohanty 1991: 56)

Metropolitan feminists were making the same kind of error that White male ethnographers often made. As Diane Bell shows in *Daughters of the Dreaming* (1983), central desert Aboriginal societies in Australia had been persistently painted as male-centred, because the ethnographers failed to collect information from Aboriginal women. Starting from the indigenous women's perspective yielded a very different picture of their traditional authority and agency. But women's situation deteriorated sharply with colonization.

Mohanty's essay was published in a collection called *Third World Women and the Politics of Feminism* (Mohanty, Russo and Torres 1991). This book had a considerable impact, both by documenting the global diversity of women's politics, and as a statement of another kind of theory. In a long introduction called 'Cartographies of struggle', and in later essays collected in *Feminism Without Borders* (2003), Mohanty spelled out an approach to gender that started with the historical experience of imperialism. The making and re-making of gender is interwoven with the making of race and the dynamic of global capitalism. Mohanty agrees with deconstructionism that there is no pre-given universal category of 'woman', but for another reason: because the all-too-real practices of domination constantly divide people. Capitalism uses local gender ideologies to incorporate 'women's work' into strategies of profit-making. This approach allows Mohanty to go a step further, to emphasize the practices of solidarity, the possibilities of common struggle, that can link the poor and the marginalized across differences.

Even better known than Mohanty's, and closer to metropolitan deconstructionism, was the work of another Indian expatriate feminist, Gayatri Chakravorty Spivak (1988, 1999). Spivak's writings on feminism are in a variety of genres and defy short summary. She would not think of herself as producing a 'theory of gender', indeed she seems to show the limits of any such project. Her most famous essay, 'Can the subaltern speak?', builds on the work of the Indian historians who founded *Subaltern Studies*, but takes apart their project of rediscovering subaltern consciousness. Her most famous concept, 'strategic essentialism', adopts the deconstructionist critique of identity categories but then sees a point to those categories in practice. In the essay where this idea emerged, Spivak performed the classic feminist action of pointing to the absences of women from a system of interpretation constructed by men.

As one of the most famous figures in post-colonial studies, Spivak commands international attention, yet constantly limits her claims. I think her work intends to be educational, rather than to state definitive positions. She wants her readers to think for themselves, to learn deconstructive methods, and at the same time to be politically engaged. She consistently calls attention to women in poverty, in extremely marginalized situations; but emphasizes the dangers of intellectuals setting themselves up to speak on behalf of dominated groups. Like Mohanty, she sees global capitalism as the connector between a variety of dominated groups. Yet it isn't easy to see how Spivak's style of work would generate political strategies commensurate with the problem.

Spivak's virtuosity with the technique of deconstruction raises a consistently difficult question – the tension between location (or origin) in the global periphery, and concepts from the metropole. Paulin Hountondji, a philosopher from Benin, has explored this issue in depth. In a key essay called 'Recentring Africa', Hountondji (1997) speaks of the 'extraversion' that is characteristic of knowledge production in the global periphery. In a global division of scientific labour, set up under colonialism but persisting in the post-colonial world, data collection and practical applications of knowledge may occur in the periphery, but the crucial step of *theorizing* occurs overwhelmingly in the metropole. Following the logic of extraversion, intellectuals in the periphery look outward to the metropole as the source of their concepts, methods, equipment, training and recognition.

A polarity thus arises between modernity, science and development, on the one hand, and traditional knowledge on the other. This cannot be overcome by simply affirming an indigenous world-view as an uncorrupted alternative to Western thought. As Hountondji and others had shown earlier, the very attempt to formulate an indigenous philosophy out of local folkways reproduced the colonizers' gaze on indigenous society, supporting nativist ideologies that could be, and are, manipulated by power-holders in the periphery. The only way out of the trap is a new relationship of critical validation between endogenous knowledge and globally circulating knowledge systems, in which both are open to critique.

What Hountondji says about the extraversion of science in the global periphery is strikingly true of gender analysis. Most research and debate on gender questions draws on gender theory from the metropole and tries to combine it with local data or experience. This was, for instance, the structure of knowledge when the All-China Federation of Women sponsored a week-long symposium on 'theoretical studies on women' in 1984, in the early days of the Chinese government's economic reforms. The idea of women's studies was borrowed from the United States, local statistics about the situation of women were compiled, and the result was an agenda for 'women's studies the Chinese way' – with a focus on women's relationship to the new economic policies (Shen 1987).

Since I have been talking about Mohanty and Spivak, I will also give an example from India. In a paper called 'Problems for a contemporary theory of gender', published in *Subaltern Studies*, Susie Tharu and

Tejaswini Niranjana (1996) discuss women's role in Indian right-wing politics, the use of women's empowerment rhetoric by contraceptive manufacturers, and a village women's temperance campaign. The theoretical problem the authors see in these cases is feminism's complicity with the universal humanist subject. That is a formulation from postmodernist feminism in the metropole. It is difficult to see as a central problem about Indian feminism, which had been grappling with communalism, class, region, rural/urban and other forms of difference for decades (Menon 1999).

The issue of extraversion and what to do about it has concerned many gender researchers in the majority world. When gender research was launched in post-colonial Africa in the 1970s, there was an attempt to locate it within African perspectives, though ideas and methods were adapted from the metropole (Arnfred 2003). There has been recent debate about whether the concept of gender itself can be applied in Africa. A major example concerns Yoruba culture in Nigeria: Oyèrónké Oyéwùmí's *The Invention of Women: Making an African Sense of Western Gender Discourses* (1997). Oyéwùmí argues that Western gender concepts are based on dichotomizing people on the basis of the body, and that this was not done in pre-colonial Oyo-Yoruba society. The language itself was gender-free, and there was no social category corresponding to the Western category of 'women'. The major organizing principle of Oyo society, she argues, was seniority, i.e. authority accorded on the basis of age, without respect to anatomical sex. Western gender categories are an intrusion, imposed on local people under colonialism. Oyéwùmí gives considerable detail of the impact of missions, the colonial state and new industries such as railways in producing a colonial version of Western gender relations. Contemporary feminism, and its gender theory, continues this cultural imperialism.

But other scholars do see gender patterns in pre-colonial Yoruba culture. Bibi Bakare-Yusuf (2003) points to misogynist Yoruba proverbs, and other cultural evidence that points to gendered patterns of power. Oyéwùmí, she argues, misinterpreted the situation by looking only at the formal properties of language, missing how language is inscribed in social practices, and how experience is embodied. The language of seniority, for instance, can mask the marginalization of many women and the abuse of youth. Colonialism certainly changed gender patterns, but it did so by building on distinctions that already existed in Yoruba culture. Bakare-Yusuf also takes a different stand on the relation of indigenous to metropolitan knowledge systems. It is a mistake, she argues, to try to reconstruct a hermetically sealed indigenous cultural system, and reject everything other as an intrusion. African cultures have always been plural, and open to otherness and change. In contemporary Africa, complex gender systems certainly do exist and have major consequences. Among them are the patterns of economic inequality, gendered violence and sexuality that shape the HIV/AIDS crisis (Ampofo, Beoku-Betts, Njambi and Osirim 2004).

The significance of gender as a structuring principle has not been in much doubt in Latin America, where debates about 'machismo' were running long before the contemporary women's movement emerged. The Mexican sociologist Teresita de Barbieri is one feminist who has tried to work out a systematic account. In an essay 'On the category of gender: a theoretical–methodological introduction' (1992), de Barbieri offers a relational model of gender, based on the central idea of social control over women's reproductive power, but involving a wide range of processes: 'practices, symbols, representations, values, collective norms'. She emphasizes that, though the figures of the woman as mother and the man as head of household are the nucleus of gender definitions in Latin America, gender is *not* a simple dichotomy. The gender system involves male/male and female/female relations as well as male/female – for instance, inequalities among women involving domestic service – as well as life-cycle shifts in gender differentiation, and conflicts of interest within gender categories, such as men who support feminist demands. Building on Black feminist thought in Brazil, de Barbieri also emphasizes how gender relations are implicated with race relations, and class divisions, in a stratified plural society.

This is not presented as a finished theory; de Barbieri is clear that gender analysis is a field open to development and debate. And of course there are many other perspectives across Latin America, some of them especially interested in how gender changes under structural adjustment and contemporary globalization. De Barbieri argued that gender research needed to include men, and this has indeed become one of the distinctive features of Latin American gender analysis. Most focused in Chile and Mexico, but also spread across the continent and the Caribbean, there is now a wealth of research and debate about masculine identity, class and race differences among men, changes in fatherhood, work and sexuality (Gutmann and Viveros Vigoya 2005).

This work has generally assumed well-formed, well-integrated gender orders – de Barbieri has no hesitation in speaking of 'gender systems' – even if they are complex and cross-cut by other social structures. Yet a focus on the societies of the global periphery raises the question of how local gender orders might be dis-integrated, by the processes of colonization, decolonization, and the pressure of a globally dominant economy and culture. Mai Ghoussoub (2000), for instance, speaks of a great cultural disturbance in the contemporary Arab world around the position and identities of men – not a settled system but 'a chaotic quest for a definition of modern masculinity'.

The Indian anthropologist Veena Das (1995) poses the question in the context of a social tragedy. When leaving India, the British colonizers divided it. Partition in 1947 was accompanied by enormous relocations of Muslim, Hindu and Sikh populations, and a great deal of communal violence. Women were targeted for rape, abduction and murder, in order to stain the opposing community – men fought each other via the bodies of women. Looking at the experience of the women caught up in this, Das observes that what happened to particular women often followed no logic at all, whether they escaped or suffered seemed random; social order as such broke down. Social analysis reaches a limit in thinking about such a situation.

In this section of the chapter I haven't tried to write a history of gender theory beyond the global metropole – only to point to some key issues that have been raised, and to suggest the richness of ideas from the global South. There is a great variety of perspectives, and there are different ways of interacting with the gender theories of the metropole. It is a little tempting to settle for the idea of multiple perspectives on gender issues, admit there are multiple truths, and leave it at that.

Reality demands more. As Latin American thinkers especially emphasize, the societies of the global periphery are constantly impacted and re-positioned by the economic and military centre. We do not live in a mosaic world where each culture is separate. Yet we are not being simply homogenized, as popular theories of globalization suppose. We need ways of talking to each other across boundaries, and that is abundantly true of gender analysis.

In *Re-Orienting Western Feminisms: Women's Diversity in a Post-colonial World* (1998), the Australian sociologist Chilla Bulbeck describes this problem and considers what is involved in moving beyond the Euro-centrism still common in feminist thought in the metropole. To respond adequately to world-wide diversity is not just a matter of tacking 'anti-racism' onto an existing agenda. The issue is deeper, concerning ways of knowing and methods of action. It is a matter of learning to see oneself as others see one, learning to respect other experiences as genuinely other, and learning to work in coalition modes. Bulbeck calls this a 'world-traveller perspective', and, provided we recognize that for the poorest nine-tenths of the world's population the world travel has to be done in the mind, that is a good image for the kind of gender theory we now need.

4

Sex differences and gendered bodies

At the centre of commonsense thinking about gender is the idea of natural difference between women and men. A whole industry of pop psychology tells us that women and men are naturally opposites in their thinking, emotions and capacities. The most popular book in this genre, which assures us that men and women are like beings from different planets, has sold *30 million* copies and is translated into 40 languages. Other books in this genre, and endless articles in popular magazines, tell us that men and women communicate in different ways, that boys and girls learn differently, that hormones make men into warriors, or that 'brain sex' rules our lives. Most of the claims in these books are, in scientific terms, complete nonsense, refuted by a mass of research evidence. The US psychologist Janet Hyde (2005), the leading authority on gender difference research, points out that the pop-psychology doctrine of natural difference is harmful to children's education, to women's employment rights and to all adults' emotional relationships. Clearly we need better ways of thinking about differences and bodies. The development of gender studies now provides some of the necessary tools.

Reproductive difference

Why is there any difference at all between women's and men's bodies? Humans share with many other species, plants as well as animals, the system of sexual reproduction – a method of reproducing which allows genetic information from two individuals to be combined, rather than just one to be copied. Sexual reproduction is itself a product of evolution, perhaps 400 million years old. Life forms existed earlier, reproducing in other ways – as many species still do. Some, including orchids and grasses, reproduce both sexually and asexually. Biologists debate why sex evolved, for this odd scheme has some evolutionary disadvantages. It may have evolved because sexual reproduction allows faster change, or prevents the accumulation of harmful mutations.

Sexual reproduction does not require bodies to be specialized by sex. Among earthworms, for instance, each individual is hermaphrodite, producing both sperm and ova (eggs), and thus every worm is able to perform both male and female functions. In other species, individuals produce either sperm or ova but not both. Their bodies are to some extent 'dimorphic', i.e. in a given species there exist two forms. Humans are among these species.

Genetic information is encoded in DNA and carried on chromosomes, microscopic structures within the nucleus of each cell in a plant or animal. The genetic information that is combined at fertilization (in sexual reproduction) comes half from a female, in the egg nucleus, and half from a male, in the sperm nucleus. Human cells have forty-six chromosomes, which come in pairs. One pair, the sex chromosomes, influences the development of the body's male and female sexual characteristics. Females have two X chromosomes in this pair, males have one X and one Y chromosome. Under the influence of the genetic information here, and given the usual environmental conditions, male and female bodies develop specialized organs – wombs, testes, breasts – and certain differences in physiology, such as the balance of hormones circulating in the blood, and the menstrual cycle in women.

Among mammals, females not only produce ova but also carry foetuses in a protective womb (except for monotremes such as the platypus, which lay eggs). They feed infants with milk from specialized organs (in humans, breasts). Among some mammal species, but not all, males have extra bulk, or extra equipment: the antlers of male deer, for instance. Humans are mammals with well-differentiated reproductive systems, but modest physical differences between sexes in other respects. Human males do not have antlers.

In several respects human bodies are not fully dimorphic. First, there are a considerable number of intersex categories, such as females lacking a second X chromosome, males with an extra X chromosome, anomalous or contradictory hormonal patterns, and a surprising variety of unstandard forms taken by the internal and external genitals. These categories have fascinated sexologists, and do not correspond in any simple way to behaviour. The biologist Anne Fausto-Sterling (2000: 51) estimates that the different intersex groups, taken together, may account for 1.7 per cent of all births: a small but not a trivial number. A collection of life stories has been published in *Intersex* by Catherine Harper (2007), with a strong critique of the rush to 'correct' these variations by surgery on small children.

Second, physical differences between male and female change over the lifespan. In the early stages of development, male and female bodies are relatively undifferentiated; there are only small differences between a two-year-old girl and a two-year-old boy. Even the visibly different external reproductive organs – penis, clitoris, scrotum and labia – develop embryonically from a common starting point. In a number of respects male and female bodies also become more similar in old age, for instance in their hormonal balance.

Third, even in early adulthood the physical characteristics of males as a group, and females as a group, overlap extensively. Height is a simple example. Adult males are on average a little taller than adult females, but the diversity of heights within each group is great, in relation to the average difference. Therefore a very large number of individual women are taller than many individual men. We tend not to notice this physical fact because of social custom. When a man and a woman form a couple, they usually pick partners who show the 'expected' difference in height.

A more complex example is the brain – the site of a great deal of recent discussion of sex differences. There are some differences in brain anatomy and functioning between women and men, for instance in the tendency to use particular areas of the brain in language processing. But the differences are fewer, and less reliably established, than aggressive popular accounts of 'brain sex' suggest. In many areas of brain anatomy and functioning, there are no significant sex differences. Where there are differences, these may be caused by different behaviours rather than causing them. Brain research now places a lot of emphasis on 'brain plasticity', the capacity of the brain to form new neural connections and lose old ones, i.e. to learn and change. As the neuroscientist Lesley Rogers (2000: 34) puts it: 'The brain does not choose neatly to be either a female or a male type. In any aspect of brain function that we can measure there is considerable overlap between females and males.' As we shall see, this is also a key point about human behaviour.

Conflicting accounts of difference

The fact of reproductive difference between male and female humans is hardly controversial, but its significance is. On this question, approaches to gender diverge sharply. Some treat the body as a kind of machine that manufactures gender difference; some treat the body as a kind of canvas on which culture paints images of gender; some try to staple the machine and canvas images together. None of these, I will argue, is a satisfactory way of understanding the problem.

In many discussions of gender, reproductive difference is assumed to be directly reflected in a whole range of other differences: bodily strength and speed (men are stronger and faster), physical skills (men have mechanical skills, women are good at fiddly work), sexual desire (men have more powerful urges), recreational interests (men love sport, women gossip), character (men are aggressive, women are nurturant), intellect (men are rational, women have intuition) and so on. It is widely believed that these differences are large, and that they are 'natural'.

The idea that natural difference provides the basis for the social pattern of gender takes many forms. One is that men dominate in society because, with their higher levels of testosterone, they have a hormonal 'aggression advantage' in competition for top jobs. Therefore society needs patriarchy – Steven Goldberg claimed in *Why Men Rule* (1993) – to protect women from failure! More complex arguments have been proposed by the US biologist Edward Wilson, who coined the term 'sociobiology', and a newer group who call their work 'evolutionary psychology'. Broadly, these arguments deduce social gender from reproductive strategies. From this vaguely Darwinian starting point, theorists have deduced human kinship loyalties, mothers' commitment to their children, husbands' sexual infidelity, women's coyness, men's interest in pornography, male bonding, and a remarkable range of other gender patterns. The 'evolutionary psychology' argument is presented in detail by David Geary in *Male, Female* (1998). Geary's aim is to link psychological research on sex differences with Darwin's concept of 'sexual selection' (the choice of mates in sexual reproduction) as a mechanism of evolution. Geary works his way through the now huge research literature on human sex differences (see below). For each topic where a sex difference can be located, Geary offers an account of how it *might* be linked to sexual selection, that is, how humans choose, win and control mates.

Models of the body as a machine producing gender difference are mainly advanced by men, and have often been used to defend the existing gender order, to ridicule feminism or feminist ideas about gender roles. However, there are also feminist arguments which present bodies as direct sources of gender difference. US feminists in the 1980s often saw male aggression and female peacefulness as natural. The terms 'male violence' and 'male sexuality', which became common at this time, implicitly linked behaviour to the body, and some activists directly identified the penis as the source of male power (a view dissected by Segal 1994).

The idea of natural difference runs into difficulties on several fronts. Sociobiological explanations of human kinship, for instance, foundered when the predictions from genetics failed to match the realities of kinship systems actually documented by anthropologists (Sahlins 1977). It seems that social logic works independently of genetic logic. The explanation of gender hierarchy by a hormonal 'aggression advantage' fails when it is discovered that higher testosterone levels *follow from* social dominance as much as they precede it (Kemper 1990). The 'evolutionary psychology' arguments are based on an unrealistic individualism, which takes no account of institutionalized gender arrangements. For instance, in discussing the higher levels of violence among men than among women, all that Geary (1998) can see is male vs male competition for reproductive resources. He cannot see military institutions, insurgencies, mafias or cultural definitions of manhood – let alone football.

But the most striking problem about sociobiology and evolutionary psychology, given the constant appeals to 'science', to evolution and to Darwin, is that the entire argument is based on speculation. Not one sex difference in psychological characteristics has actually been *shown* to result from evolutionary mechanisms.

It is clear that bodies are affected by social processes. The way our bodies grow and function is influenced by food distribution, sexual customs, warfare, work, sport, urbanization, education and medicine, to name only the most obvious influences. And *all* these influences are structured by gender. So we cannot think of social gender arrangements as just flowing from the properties of bodies. They also precede bodies, form the conditions in which bodies develop and live. There is, as Celia Roberts (2000) puts it, a co-construction of the biological and the social.

Starkly opposed to the body-as-machine is the idea of the body as a canvas on which culture paints images of womanhood and manhood. Second-wave feminism was very much concerned with the way women's bodies were represented and moulded. One of the very first Women's Liberation demonstrations was against the Miss America beauty pageant at Atlantic City in 1968. (Contrary to an almost universal media myth, no bras were burned at this demonstration. Rather, bras and other constricting underclothes were thrown into a Freedom Trash Can.) Research on gender imagery is one of the great accomplishments of Women's Studies as an academic field. Historical research such as Lois Banner's *American Beauty* (1983) traces the shifting but powerful systems of signs through which women's bodies are defined as elegant, beautiful and desirable, or unfashionable and ugly. The imagery of men's bodies has come in for more recent scrutiny. A nice example is Dorinne Kondo's (1999) study which looks at the advertising campaign through which a

Japanese manufacturer of expensive suits created an appeal to a supposed Japanese aesthetic, embodied by the elite of salarymen who stalked around in their particular brand.

Analyses of the imagery of women's bodies in film, television, photography and other visual arts have reached high levels of sophistication, and have fed into mainstream art criticism. An excellent example is *Modern Boy Modern Girl* (Menzies 1998), a show which traced the interplay between modernist art and gender change in an earlier period of Japanese history. The 1920s saw the emergence of a new individualism and the images of 'mobo' and 'moga' (modern boy and modern girl) in the public spaces of Tokyo.

Recent cultural studies of the body often focus on language or discourse, under the influence of the French historian Michel Foucault. In a number of celebrated studies, most completely in *Discipline and Punish* (1977), Foucault showed how modern systems of knowledge had come to sort people into categories, and how these categories were interwoven with techniques of social discipline that policed their bodies. A key role was played by professions such as medicine, psychology and criminology, which applied these techniques in an amalgam that Foucault calls power/knowledge (it rhymes in French: *pouvoir-savoir*). Foucault, notoriously, failed to theorize gender, though most of his stuff is actually about men in masculinized institutions. However, his approach was taken up by many post-structuralist feminists (Fraser 1989), and is readily turned into a theory of gender by treating gendered bodies as the products of disciplinary practices. The effects are material; bodies are 'docile' and biology bends to the hurricane of social discipline.

Field research shows how such disciplining is done. The Los Angeles body-building gyms studied by the ethnographer Alan Klein (1993) show a whole sub-culture of men subjected to a fierce regime of exercise, diet and drugs. Over years of subjection to this regime their bodies are sculpted into the ideal masculine forms desired in body-building competitions.

This is an extreme case, but more moderate disciplining of bodies is very widespread. It is undertaken by such powerful institutions as sport, education and medicine. The introduction of 'physical training' in public school systems, traced in Australia by David Kirk (1993) and in the Netherlands by Mineke van Essen (2000), created schemes for training boys' and girls' bodies differently. Modern physical education is interwoven with competitive sport, and there is now impressive documentation of the gendered character of sports institutions. Nancy Theberge (1991) shows how the different exercise regimes for men and women, the disciplinary practices that both teach and constitute sports, are designed to produce gendered bodies. Michael Messner (2007) has shown, through a long research programme, how pervasive gender stereotyping and gender inequality are in the US sports world.

And if social discipline cannot produce gendered bodies, the knife can. The silicon breast implant scandal made public the scale on which cosmetic surgery has been done in the United States, where big breasts are thought sexy. This whole industry, one might think, flies in the face of the ideology of natural difference. Research on cosmetic surgeons and their clients by Diana Dull and Candace West (1991) shows a startling solution. Cosmetic surgery is now considered 'natural' for a woman, but not for a man. The exception is penile surgery, where penis enlargement is now a considerable business – as millions of spam messages on the Internet show.

Body-canvas approaches, though they have been wonderfully productive, also run into difficulty. The approach emphasizes the signifier to the point where the signified practically vanishes. With gender, the difficulty is crucial. What makes a symbolic structure a gender structure, rather than some other kind, is the fact that its signs refer eventually to the reproductive distinction between women and men.

This is not to say that all gender relations are intended to produce children. Far from it! Even most heterosexual sexuality does not result in pregnancy. Homosexual relations too are gendered. As Rosemary Pringle (1992: 91) commented, 'Whether you went to bed with a man or a woman continued to matter!' Gender involves a lot more than one-to-one relationships between bodies; it involves a vast and complicated institutional and cultural order. It is this whole order that comes into relation with bodies, and gives them gender meanings. Post-structuralist theory acknowledges that order, but often exaggerates the docility of bodies. Bodies may participate in disciplinary regimes not because they are docile, but because they are active. They seek pleasure, seek experience, seek transformation. Some startling examples of this can be found in contemporary sadomasochist sexual sub-cultures. People submit to corsets, chains, piercing, branding, rope bondage, and a whole spectrum of painfully restrictive clothes in rubber and leather – voluntarily, indeed with delight, as Valerie Steele shows in *Fetish* (1996). The same is surely true, in milder forms, of the whole system of fashion. Nobody compels young women to wear shoes with stiletto heels; they hurt after a few minutes, and they wreak havoc after a few years, but they are, also, enjoyable.

Bodies are also recalcitrant and difficult. In *The Men and the Boys* (Connell 2000), I give some case studies of this. One is a young man whose driven performance of masculinity – partying, drinking, screwing around, taking cocktails of drugs, etc. – came to an end because the resilience of his body came to an end; he became very sick. Another is a man whose un-athletic body triggered a sense of difference which became sexual difference, emerging in a homosexual identity. The issue is imaginatively explored in Patrick White's great novel *The Twyborn Affair* (1979). This story centres on the experience of Eddie/Eudoxia, whose body cannot settle into any of the gendered locations intended for it – as husband, wife, soldier, pastoralist or, ultimately, madam of a brothel.

Bodies also labour. Work is a material practice in which bodies are deployed and consumed, and gender meanings arise from this materiality. The point is forcibly made in studies of men in industries such as construction and steelmaking. The masculinity of industrial labour in these settings consists in its heaviness, risk and difficulty, where men put themselves 'in harm's way', as a vivid US ethnographic study of the construction industry puts it (Paap 2006). These are ways that bodies are consumed: worn down, injured, sometimes killed. As Mike Donaldson (1991) remarks, 'the very destruction of the physical site of masculinity, the body, can be a method of attaining, demonstrating and perpetuating the socially masculine'. Donaldson's point applies even more forcibly to the horrifying business of demonstrating masculinity by dismembering bodies in war.

Bodies cannot be understood as just the objects of social process, whether symbolic or disciplinary. They are active participants in social process. They participate through their capacities, development and needs, through the friction of their recalcitrance, and through the directions set by their pleasures and skills. Bodies must be seen as sharing in social agency, in generating and shaping courses of social conduct. Yet all the difficulties of biological determinism, outlined above, remain. Can we solve these problems by holding both a machine and a canvas image of the gendered body at the same time?

In the 1970s a number of feminist theorists did exactly this, proposing a sharp distinction between 'sex' and 'gender'. Sex was the biological fact, the difference between the male and the female human animal. Gender was the social fact, the difference between masculine and feminine roles, or men's and women's personalities.

To many at the time, this two-realms model was a conceptual breakthrough, showing why biology could not be used to justify women's subordination. The constraints of biological difference were confined to the realm of biology itself. A broad realm of the social ('culture', 'roles', etc.) remained, a realm of freedom, where individuals or societies could choose the gender patterns they wanted. Eleanor Maccoby and Carol Jacklin, the authors of a vast and influential survey of *The Psychology of Sex Differences* (1975), concluded:

We suggest that societies have the option of minimizing, rather than maximizing, sex differences through their socialization practices. A society could, for example, devote its energies more toward moderating male aggression than toward preparing women to submit to male aggression, or toward encouraging rather than discouraging male nurturance activities.

The concept of 'androgyny' put forward by Sandra Bem (1974) and other psychologists at this time was a popular attempt to define an alternative gender pattern, a mixture of masculine and feminine characteristics, which an individual or a society could choose. Quantitative psychologists since then have continued to add complexities to the picture of sex roles. For instance, James Mahalik and colleagues (2003), creating a large 'conformity to masculine norms' questionnaire and putting it through a statistical factor analysis, find no less than eleven dimensions, which they take to represent different masculine 'norms' co-existing among US college students. However, Andrew Smiler's (2004) excellent history of masculinity scales concludes ruefully that all this effort has had little impact on mainstream psychology, which continues to treat 'sex' as a simple dichotomy.

At the high tide of North American liberal feminism in the 1970s, the two-realms model supported an optimistic, even sunny, view of change. Oppressive gender arrangements, being the products of past choices, could be abolished by fresh choices. In the language of the day, sex role expectations could be altered, and sex role socialization would follow suit.

Whole reform agendas were constructed around this principle. Among them were media reforms (to change sex role models), educational reforms (to change the expectations transmitted to girls and boys) and new forms of psychotherapy (to help individuals make the change to new roles). A notable example is the pioneering Australian Schools Commission's report *Girls, School and Society* (1975). This described the ways girls were held back by restrictive social stereotypes, and proposed action to break down educational segregation and widen girls' job choices. From this report flowed a series of projects in Australian schools encouraging girls to work in areas such as mathematics, science and technology.

However, the two-realms model soon ran into trouble, as Rosemary Pringle (1992) shows in a careful critique. The idea of gender as culturally chosen difference ('sex roles') was unable to explain why one side of that difference, the masculine, was consistently more highly valued than the other. The separation of gender from bodies ran counter to developments in feminism which were placing stronger emphasis on bodies. These developments included the growing concern with men's violence and heterosexual sexuality, whose target is not a feminine role but women's bodies.

At the same time there was a growing influence of French theorists who highlighted bodies as the objects of social power and the sources of emotion and symbolism. Some Anglophone feminist philosophers influenced by this school, such as Elizabeth Grosz (1994), insist there is no consistent distinction between body and mind, and that our embodiment itself is adequate to explain our subjectivity.

If the two realms cannot be held strictly apart, perhaps they can be added together? A commonsense compromise would suggest that gender differences arise from *both* biology and social norms.

This additive conception underlies most discussions of gender in social psychology, where the term 'sex role' is still widely used. This very phrase adds together a biological and a dramaturgical term. Similarly, moderate sociobiologists (e.g. Degler 1990) assume that there is some social elaboration of the biological differences they believe in: for instance, that boys' natural aggressiveness is socially channelled into football, war or peanut marketing.

But there are difficulties in the additive conception too. The two levels of analysis are not easily comparable. In such discussions, it is almost always assumed that biology's reality is more real than sociology's, its explanations more powerful, and its categories more fixed. To take just one example, the passage from Maccoby and Jacklin quoted above continues, saying (ungrammatically) 'A variety of social institutions are viable within the framework set by biology.' Maccoby and Jacklin argue for social choice, and want change, but the causal priority in their analysis is clear. Biology determines; only within its 'framework' may humans choose their gender arrangements.

Sex role theory and sex difference research constantly collapse into biological dichotomy. It is striking that the same occurs in the 'corporeal feminism' proposed by Grosz, who strongly rejects the mind/body dichotomy. Bodies – a little surprisingly, given that her well-known book is called *Volatile Bodies* – at the end of the analysis are starkly either male or female. So the corporeal subjectivity she outlines is necessarily sex-specific.

A further difficulty is that the patterns of difference at the two levels need not match. As we have seen already, human bodies are dimorphic only in limited ways. On the other side, human behaviour is hardly dimorphic at all, even in areas closely related to sexual reproduction. For instance, while few men do child care with infants, it is also true that, at any given time, most women are not doing this work either.

In current social life, there is a whole spectrum of gender variations. In *Breaking the Bowls* (2005), the US sociologist Judith Lorber observes that, for any individual, gender is composed of: sex category; gender identity; gendered marital and procreative status; gendered sexual orientation; gendered personality; gender processes (in everyday interaction); gender beliefs; and gender display. Since there is variety in most of these elements, the number of available gender positions rises into the hundreds, perhaps into the thousands. So much for dimorphism!

There are times when, as additive theories propose, social processes do elaborate on bodily difference. The Wonderbra springs to mind. But there are other times when social process distorts, contradicts, complicates, minimizes or modifies bodily difference. As Thorne's study (chapter 2 above) shows, life in an elementary school may do several of these things in turn, in the course of an ordinary day.

It is impossible to sustain a two-realms model of gender difference, any more than we can sustain the machine or canvas models. It is time to look more closely at the evidence about difference itself.

Facts about difference: 'sex similarity' research

In pop psychology, bodily differences and social effects are linked through the idea of *character dichotomy*. Women are supposed to have one set of traits, men another. Women are supposed to be nurturant, suggestible, talkative, emotional, intuitive and sexually loyal; men are supposed to be aggressive, tough-minded, taciturn, rational, analytic and promiscuous. These ideas have been strong in Western culture since the nineteenth century, when the belief that women had weaker intellects and less capacity for judgement than men was used to justify their exclusion from universities and from the vote.

Women have now entered universities and polling-booths, but the belief in character dichotomy remains strong. This is occasionally to women's advantage. For instance, it is often argued that there should be more women in management and government because they will bring their distinctive traits, e.g. empathy and relationship skills, to these tasks. (Research shows that senior women in management actually behave like senior men.) More often, the idea of character dichotomy is to men's advantage. Examples are the belief that women can't be top managers because they lack the necessary aggressiveness and analytical skills; or the belief that when men engage in predatory or selfish sexual conduct they are only doing what is natural for men and cannot be expected to change.

The belief in character dichotomy was one of the first issues about gender to be addressed in empirical research. Starting in the 1890s, generations of psychologists have measured various traits with tests or scales, and compared the results for women with those for men. This body of research, long known as 'sex difference' (sometimes 'gender difference') research, is huge; this is one of the most-researched topics in psychology. There is also a large parallel literature in sociology and political science, looking at group gender differences in attitudes and opinions, voting, violence and so forth.

The beginning of this research is described in a fascinating historical study by Rosalind Rosenberg, *Beyond Separate Spheres* (1982). The first generation of psychological researchers found, contrary to mainstream Victorian belief, that the mental capacities of men and women were more or less equal. It is an interesting fact that this finding of 'no difference' was rapidly accepted by men as well as women in the mental-testing field. Indeed, as they developed standardized tests of general ability or intelligence (the so-called IQ tests) during the first half of the twentieth century, psychologists incorporated the 'no difference' finding as a given, choosing and scoring test items in such a way that males and females would have equal average scores. Later attempts to find gender differences in this field have come to nothing (Halpern and LaMay 2000). It is now widely accepted that, in general intelligence, there are no significant gender differences.

An even more interesting fact is that this is the usual finding in the gender difference research as a whole. In table after table of Maccoby and Jacklin's book, the commonest entry in the column for the finding about difference is 'none'. Study after study, on trait after trait, comparing women's results with men's or girls' with boys', finds no significant difference. In summarizing their findings, the first thing Maccoby and Jacklin (1975: 349) did was list a series of 'Unfounded beliefs about sex differences'. On the evidence they compiled, it is *not* true that girls are more social than boys, that girls are more suggestible than boys, that girls have lower self-esteem, that girls are better at rote learning and boys at higher-level cognitive processing, that boys are more analytic, that girls are more affected by heredity and boys by environment, that girls lack achievement motivation, or that girls are auditory while boys are visual. All these beliefs turn out to be myths.

Maccoby and Jacklin were not alone in this conclusion. For instance Hugh Fairweather (1976), after an extensive examination of the research on gender differences in cognitive skills, concluded that gender differences were too few and uncertain to be worth bothering about. When I came to review this literature in the 1980s, it was obvious that, despite the intention to study difference:

In fact the main finding, from about eighty years of research, is a massive psychological *similarity* between women and men in the populations studied by psychologists. Clear-cut block differences are few, and confined to restricted topics. Small differences-on-average, in the context of a very large overlapping of the distributions of men and women, are usual even with traits where differences appear fairly consistently. If it were not for the cultural bias of both writers and readers, we might long ago have been talking about this as 'sex similarity' research. (Connell 1987: 170)

It is therefore intensely interesting to find that this conclusion is widely disbelieved. The acceptance of gender similarity in the field of intelligence testing turns out to have been exceptional. Pop psychology is utterly committed to the idea of difference. In the academic world, generations of researchers, in the teeth of the evidence their own disciplines have produced, have gone on relentlessly searching for, and writing about, psychological gender differences.

The gap between the main pattern actually found, and the widespread belief about what *should* be found, is so great that Cynthia Epstein (1988) entitled her admirable book about dichotomous thinking and gender reality *Deceptive Distinctions*. Two decades later, when she was president of the American Sociological Association, Epstein (2007) was still having to argue against the conventional 'master narrative' that holds 'that men and women are naturally different and have different intelligences, physical abilities, and emotional traits'.

Why the huge reluctance to accept the evidence of similarity? A large part of the explanation, I am sure, lies in the cultural background. Dichotomous gender symbolism is very strong in Western culture, so it is not surprising that when researchers look at sex and gender, what they 'see' is difference. Within our usual research design, gender similarity is not a positive state; it is merely the absence of proven difference (literally, the 'null hypothesis'). Epstein gives an example of journal editors not liking to publish null results; so the true evidence for gender similarity may be *even stronger* than the published literature reveals. Nature abhors a vacuum, and so do researchers; true difference might always be revealed by improved methods; so, one goes on searching for ever . . . This way, madness lies.

But are the facts as solid as they seem? Conventional psychological tests, it is sometimes said, are too superficial to detect the underlying patterns of gender. The real character differences between women and men may be lodged at a deeper level in personality – say, in the unconscious (as in the Jungian dichotomy of the 'deep masculine' and the 'deep feminine'). This could be true. Certainly most quantitative tests in psychology measure only the immediately apparent aspects of behaviour, often through self-report. But if the 'deep' differences don't show up at the level of everyday life, and keep on failing to show up across a wide range of behaviours – which is what the quantitative research showed – then one wonders how important such deep differences really can be.

A second issue is that the finding of 'no difference' is not uniform. Maccoby and Jacklin also pointed to a small number of traits where gender differences *did* exist, according to the bulk of their evidence: verbal ability, visual-spatial ability, mathematical ability and aggressiveness. It was these findings, not the larger 'no difference' finding, which went into the textbooks, and have been emphasized and debated by most subsequent writers.

A third issue concerns research method. Maccoby and Jacklin had a large amount of data, but most of it came from hundreds of small studies with ill-defined samples. It may be that the number of 'no difference' findings reflects the methodological weakness of the individual studies. If a way could be found to strengthen the method by combining the results of many studies, the picture might change.

Exactly this became possible when a new statistical procedure, known as 'meta-analysis', was introduced to gender difference research in the 1980s. The procedure relies on finding a large number of separate studies of the same issue: for instance, many studies attempting to measure gender differences in aggression, or intelligence, or self-esteem. In meta-analysis each study (rather than each person) is taken as one data point, and the task is to make a statistical analysis of the whole set of studies.

Obviously, before this can be done, their findings have to be expressed on a common scale. Unless all the studies have used exactly the same measurement procedures (which in practice is rarely the case), this is a problem. The ingenious solution is to define a common scale based on the variability of individual scores in the original studies.

The usual procedure in gender difference meta-analysis is this. For each study, the difference between the average scores of women and men (on whatever test is being used) is obtained, and this is rewritten as a fraction of the overall variation in people's scores found in that study on that same test. (Technically, the difference between means is divided by the mean within-group standard deviation.) This resembles a familiar way of standardizing scores in psychological measurement. The standardized gender difference, known as 'd', found for each individual study is the measurement taken forward into the meta-analysis. The unfortunate convention is that d values above zero indicate that the men's average is higher, values below zero indicate that the women's average is higher.

In the meta-analysis proper, the d scores for all the studies are examined as a group. An average d score is computed, which is usually called the 'effect size' for that group of studies. A check is made whether the group of d scores is homogeneous – so tightly clustered that probably only one underlying effect is present. If it is not, then the studies can be classified into sub-groups, and statistical checks are run on the influence of 'moderator' variables. For instance, the researcher might check whether the effect size differs between older and newer studies (which would suggest that the size of gender differences is changing over time), or between studies of different age groups, and so on.

The first impact of meta-analysis was to revive confidence in the existence and importance of gender differences generally, as can be seen in Alice Eagly's *Sex Differences in Social Behavior* (1987). Even when most studies in a group individually show non-significant differences, meta-analysis may find an effect size significantly different from zero in the group as a whole. A few examples from the many effect sizes reported are: +.21 across 216 studies of self-esteem (Kling, Hyde, Showers and Buswell, 1999), –.28 across 160 studies of 'care orientation' in moral choice (Jaffee and Hyde 2000), zero across 22 studies of 'meaning orientation' in learning styles (Severiens and ten Dam 1998), +.48 across 83 studies of aggression (Hyde 1984).

The question then arises, what do these effect sizes mean? An effect may be significantly different from zero, which means it is not a result of pure chance, but may still be so small that it does not tell us much about the world. And here meta-analysis has its limits. By convention, an effect size of .20 is called 'small', .50 is called 'medium', and .80 is called 'large'. But there is debate about how to interpret this convention. Eagly (1987) argued that even small effects may be practically important, but other meta-analysts are less convinced. Kristen Kling and her colleagues (1999) tried to get a handle on this issue by comparing their gender difference effect size with the effect sizes that have consequences in other types of research on self-esteem. They conclude that 'the gender difference in self-esteem is small when compared against effect sizes that have been shown to have important consequences in the laboratory'.

As meta-analyses built up, so did a renewed scepticism about the size and scope of gender differences. Maccoby and Jacklin in the 1970s considered that 'verbal ability' was one of the traits where a difference (favouring women) was definitely established. But Hyde and McKinley (1997), reviewing meta-analyses of research since then, report effect sizes clustering around zero. Mathematics ability, another claimed area of difference (favouring men), proves to have only a very small effect size, +.15, across 254 studies.

In 2005 Janet Hyde published a meta-survey of meta-analyses, combining the findings of this technique across the whole field of psychology. She found 46 published meta-analyses of gender difference, which analysed over 5,000 research studies, which in turn were based on the testing of about 7 million people. The research covered cognitive variables, communication, social and personality variables, psychological well-being, motor behaviours and assorted other topics. The overall finding is simply stated:

> The striking result is that 30 per cent of the effect sizes are in the close-to-zero range, and an additional 48 per cent are in the small range. That is, 78 per cent of gender differences are small or close to zero. (Hyde 2005: 582, 586)

Hyde provocatively titles her paper 'The gender similarities hypothesis'. I wouldn't call it a hypothesis, exactly. The idea of a character dichotomy between women and men has been overwhelmingly, decisively, refuted. *The broad psychological similarity of men and women as groups can be regarded, on the volume of evidence supporting it, as one of the best-established generalizations in all the human sciences.*

Hyde also recognizes that there are some traits on which average gender differences do persistently show up. In her review they include physical performances (e.g. in throwing); some aspects of sexuality, but not all; and some aspects of aggression.

What is particularly interesting in the new meta-analytic studies is that when clear psychological gender differences do appear, they are likely to be specific and situational rather than generalized. Studies of aggression often show a gender difference – but in physical aggression more than in verbal aggression, and not in all circumstances. Bettencourt and Miller (1996) find an overall d of +.22 in experimental studies of aggression, but report that this effect depends on whether or not there are conditions of provocation. Unprovoked, men have a modest tendency to show higher levels of aggressiveness than women (mean effect size +.33); provoked, men's and women's reactions are similar (mean effect size +.17). Hyde cites a meta-analysis of gender differences in making interruptions in conversation. The effect size varied, according to the type of interruption, the size of the group talking together, and whether they were strangers or friends. She comments: 'Here, again, it is clear that gender differences can be created, erased, or reversed, depending on the context' (Hyde 2005: 589).

Meta-analysis reveals that gender differences in masculinity/femininity, as measured by tests like the 'Bem Sex Role Inventory', change over time. Twenge (1997) showed that men and women (in samples of US undergraduates) became more similar in their responses on these scales over a period of twenty years, from the 1970s to the 1990s. Not, as many people fear, because men are becoming feminized – both groups' scores on the femininity scales changed little. It was rather because the women increased their scores markedly (and men a little) on masculinity scales over this period.

Meta-analysis has not entirely revolutionized the study of gender difference, since the basic data collection methods remain the same. But it has certainly clarified what this body of research is saying. Confirming earlier conclusions, it tells us that, across a wide range of the traits and characteristics measured by psychology, sharp gender differences are rare; broad similarity between women and men is the main pattern. Meta-analysis adds a clearer recognition that specific and situational sex differences often appear. Very specific skills (e.g. in one science rather than another), specific social circumstances (e.g. provocation), specific times and places (e.g. US colleges in the 1990s) and specific ways of measuring traits, all affect the extent of gender differences recorded in the research.

We thus get a picture of psychological gender differences and similarities, not as fixed, age-old constants of the species, but as the varying products of the active responses people make to a complex and changing social world. With the aid of meta-analysis, psychology has gradually moved towards the way of understanding gender that has also gradually emerged in sociology.

How far can we generalize this picture? It is often observed that the modern science of psychology is mainly based on the behaviour of White middle-class students in Psychology 101 courses in US universities – not exactly a representative sample of humanity.

Given the impressive evidence of cultural and historical variations in gender arrangements (see chapters 2 and 5), we cannot simply assume that the psychological patterns documented for the contemporary United States hold true across the world. Yet this very point, that gender differences can vary between different circumstances, has been emerging from meta-analytic research. The gender similarity research now includes increasing numbers of large-scale studies with better samples of the population of Western countries, and increasing numbers of studies in other parts of the world. I think the conclusions outlined above are a solid starting point for understanding the psychology of gender.

Social embodiment and the reproductive arena

Now that gender similarity research has decisively refuted the concept of character dichotomy, we must reject all models of gender that assume

social gender differences to be caused by bodily differences producir
character differences. How, then, can we understand the relation between
body and society in gender?

Bodies have agency *and* bodies are socially constructed. Biological and
social analysis cannot be cut apart from each other. But neither can be
reduced to the other. Within a 'difference' framework, these conclusions
sit as paradoxes. We must move towards another framework.

There are many, many differences among the 7,000 million human
bodies in the world. There are old and young, sick and well, plump and
starving. There are differences of physical ability and disability. There
are skins permanently stained with soil and skins softened with expensive
creams; hands cracked from washing and hands spotless and manicured.
Each body has its trajectory through time, each changes as it grows older.
Some bodies encounter accident, traumatic childbirth, violence, starvation, disease or surgery, and have to reorganize themselves to carry
on. Some do not survive these encounters.

Yet the tremendous multiplicity of bodies is in no sense a random
assortment. Our bodies are interconnected through social practices, the
things people do in daily life.

Bodies are both *objects of* social practice and *agents in* social practice.
The same bodies, at the same time, are both. The practices in which
bodies are involved form social structures and personal trajectories,
which in turn provide the conditions of new practices in which bodies
are addressed and involved. There is a loop, a circuit, linking bodily
processes and social structures. In fact, there is a tremendous number of
such circuits. They occur in historical time, and change over time. They
add up to the historical process in which society is embodied, and bodies
are drawn into history.

I call this process *social embodiment*. From the point of view of the
body, it could be called 'body-reflexive practice' – that is, human social
conduct in which bodies are both agents and objects.

Bodies have a reality that cannot be reduced; they are drawn into
history without ceasing to be bodies. They do not turn into signs or
positions in discourse (though discourses constantly refer to them). Their
materiality continues to matter. We are born, we are mortal. If you prick
us, do we not bleed?

Social embodiment involves an individual's conduct, but also may
involve a group, an institution or a whole complex of institutions. Consider the body-reflexive practice that goes into making the exemplary
masculinity of a sports star – for instance Steve, a champion in 'iron
man' surf competitions, whose life I describe in *The Men and the
Boys* (Connell 2000). Steve's practice includes the training routines
worked out by coaches, drawing on the professional expertise of physical

education and sports medicine. It includes the practice of the sport itself, which is organized by multi-million-dollar corporations. It includes participating in publicity and managing finance via other corporations (commercial media, advertisers). A major sports star, like other media figures, practically turns into a one-person corporation, employing lawyers, accountants, marketing agents and public relations flacks. There is an elaborate social process here, as the US sociologist Michael Messner (2007) has shown in a wide-ranging and influential programme of research on gender in sports. Yet as we see in Steve's case, all of this institutional activity and specialized work is based on, and refers back to, bodily performances.

Gender is a specific form of social embodiment. Gender relations form a particular social structure, refer to particular features of bodies, and gender practices form a circuit between them.

The distinctive feature of gender (compared with other patterns of social embodiment) is that it refers to the bodily structures and processes of human reproduction. Gender involves a cluster of human social practices – including child care, birthing, sexual interaction – which deploy human bodies' capacities to engender, to give birth, to give milk, to give and receive sexual pleasure. We can only begin to understand gender if we understand how closely the social and the bodily processes mesh. We are born in blood and pain, *and* we are born in a social order.

These bodily capacities, and the practices that realize them, constitute an arena, a bodily site where something social happens. Among the things that happen is the creation of the cultural categories 'women' and 'men' (and any other gender categories that a particular society marks out). I will call this the *reproductive arena* in social life. At the beginning of the chapter I noted that we are one of the species that reproduce sexually, and this is where that fact becomes central for gender analysis.

Nevertheless I make a strong distinction between the idea of a 'reproductive arena' and the traditional idea of a 'biological base', a natural mechanism that produces automatic social effects. Sexual reproduction does not cause gender practice, or even provide a template for it. There are many fields where strongly gendered behaviour occurs that has not the slightest logical connection with sexual reproduction. (Football, shoe design, futures markets, lesbian sex, Handel oratorios, the appointment of bishops . . .) We may be one of many species that reproduce sexually, but we are the only one of them that has produced complex, historically changing social structures in which that reproductive capacity is deployed and transformed. Gender, in fact, is one of the most striking things that is unique about our species.

What we must recognize about gender, though it is often forgotten in the excitement of gender politics among adults, is that the reproductive arena very much concerns children. Not all sex results in pregnancy, of course – in fact the great majority of sexual encounters, even heterosexual ones, don't, and aren't intended to. But the fact that children do arrive this way, and have to be nurtured and taught, and will become the next generation of parents, matters immensely for any society that intends to last much beyond next Thursday. The way caring for children is organized is a large part of the domain of gender.

The reproductive arena can be reshaped by social processes. Indeed, it constantly is being re-shaped in social struggle. For instance, the fertility of a woman's body means something different, where contraception is effective and small families are planned, from what it means where women are designated lifelong breeders and nurturers – barefoot, pregnant and in the kitchen, as the saying goes.

The reproductive arena is always the point of reference in gender processes, but it is far from incorporating everything that gender is about. We also need a concept which I will call the *gender domain*, which refers to the whole terrain of social life that is socially linked to the reproductive arena, in which relations among people and groups are structured by this linkage and can therefore be understood as gender relations.

It follows from this definition that the scope and shape of the gender domain varies from one society to another, and from one period of history to another. It can even be changed by deliberate action. This is attempted in the strategy of 'de-gendering' that some organizations follow in the belief that it will make them more efficient or fair, and that some feminists see as a general reform strategy (Connell 2006, Lorber 2005). The attempt to get more men as teachers into early childhood education in rich countries is a current, though so far not very successful, case. (In poorer countries there are already more men in elementary teaching.)

A few short examples of social embodiment in the gender domain may help illustrate what is meant. One of the crudest ways of deploying gender is through sexual harassment – an exercise of power, directed to the body of the target. Meredith Newman and her colleagues (2003) report survey evidence from employees of the US government, showing 25 per cent of women report having been sexually harassed on the job, compared with 6 per cent of men. There was little variation from one government agency to another.

In a survey of men's health research in Australia (Connell et al. 1999), one of the strongest gender differences appeared in a study of rural people's eyes. Of the patients with penetrating eye injuries, 88 per cent were men. This is not because men's eyes have weaker surfaces than women's. It is because women in rural Australia are rarely given jobs involving hammering on metal or stretching fencing wire, the main sources of this kind of injury. It is the gender division of labour that is crucial to understanding these effects – but it is the bodies that bear them.

Miriam Glucksmann's (1990) historical study of women in the electrical engineering and food processing industries in inter-war Britain shows that gender segregation was introduced in the new factories on a massive scale. Nothing about the workers' bodies, nor about the technology of chocolate biscuit production, required segregation, but women's and men's bodies were sharply separated. The reason was that to have integrated the workplace would have broken down the existing social dependence of women and the gender division of child care and housework in the workers' homes.

The deadly human immunodeficiency virus has been spread around the world by contacts between human bodies, often following gendered paths. Purnima Mane and Peter Aggleton (2001), surveying the role of men in this process, note that men's practices in different regions are shaped by local gender orders – the risk of transmission being highest where women have least capacity to control sexuality – and by prevailing definitions of manhood, for instance the acceptance of risk, the idea of proving manhood by sexual experimentation, etc. Again, the consequences of gender practices are borne in bodies, both male and female.

Bodies are transformed in social embodiment. Some broad changes in recent history are familiar: numbers of children born, lengthening expectation of life, rising average height and weight (as child nutrition and health care improve) and changing patterns of disease (e.g. polio declining, tuberculosis declined but now reviving). The transformation of bodies is structured, in part, on gender lines, as the demographic indicators show. In the rich industrial countries, women's average life expectancy is now noticeably longer than men's. In 2005, the average expectation of life for women was eighty-six years, for men seventy-nine. But in Pakistan, the figure for women is sixty-five years, and for men sixty-four; in Uganda, for women fifty, and for men forty-nine.

The idea of social embodiment, involving long circuits of practice, allows us to recognize a paradoxical aspect of gender. Many gender processes involve bodily processes and capacities that are themselves not gender-differentiated, that are in fact common capacities of women and men. For instance there are almost no gender differences of any consequence in capacities to work in an industrial economy, apart from those created by different training, the treatment of pregnancy as a disability, or the gendered design of equipment. Most production processes involve the cooperation of very large numbers of men and women in an intricate flow of work. Ironically, this shared labour creates the means through which images of gender difference are circulated. The Super Bowl, the faces of the latest supermodel and Hollywood hunk, the advertisements for cosmetics and beers, go out around the world in their hundreds of millions only because of the shared work of the women and men who build the TV sets, make the paper and keep the media corporations running.

Recognizing social embodiment also allows a new view of the relation between bodies and change in gender. In sociobiology, sex role theory, liberal feminism and popular ideologies of natural difference, bodily difference is understood to be a conservative force. It holds back historical change, limits what social action can accomplish. But we can now see that bodies as agents in social practice are involved in the very construction of the social world, the bringing-into-being of social reality. Bodies' needs, bodily desire and bodily capacities are at work in history. The social world is never simply reproduced. It is always reconstituted by practice.

Gender as a system of relations is constituted in this historical process, and accordingly can never be fixed, nor exactly reproduced. The strategic question is not 'Can gender change?' but 'In what direction is gender changing?' Any situation admits of a range of possible responses.

It is possible for social practice to move gender orders in different directions, and create different connections between bodies and social structures. The liberal-feminist idea expressed in the quotation from Maccoby and Jacklin, that a society can choose the gender order it wants, is sociologically naive. A society divided by conflicting interests does not 'choose' as a unit. But Maccoby and Jacklin were right in seeing a range of historical possibilities in gender relations. There are different futures towards which contemporary societies might be moved. I will return to this issue in chapters 5 and 8.

5

Gender relations

Patterns in gender: structure and change

The research projects discussed in chapter 2 included two studies of organizations, Barrie Thorne's study of American elementary schools and Dunbar Moodie's study of South African mines. Each of these organizations had a regular set of arrangements about gender: who was recruited to do what work (e.g. all of the mineworkers were men); what social divisions were recognized (e.g. creating 'opposite sides' in the playground); how emotional relations were conducted (e.g. the 'mine wives'); and how these institutions were related to others (e.g. the families of the workers).

Such a pattern in gender arrangements may be called the *gender regime* of an institution. Research on a very wide range of organizations has mapped their gender regimes – schools, offices, factories, armies, police forces, sporting clubs. It is clear that gender regimes are a usual feature of organizational life, and also that gender regimes change. I will take an example from my own research (Connell 2007), a study of gender patterns across ten public-sector worksites in the state of New South Wales, Australia. Well-defined gender regimes could be found in all of them: most managers were men, most technical workers were men, most clerical workers were women, most human service workers were women. At the same time, change in gender patterns was going on. Relatively widespread changes include the automation of masculinized industrial jobs, the disappearance of the 'secretary' as a well-defined occupation, and the acceptance of 'equal opportunity' as a principle. A middle-aged man whom we interviewed summed up his experience this way:

> I would like to think we are a little bit more enlightened now. I think it has been proven that women can do just about any job that a male can do, that there is no male-dominated industries as such – maybe the construction industry is. But I think that from an Agency viewpoint and even from a workplace viewpoint now, it is accepted that we have got women [professional staff], they can come in and do just as good a job as what men can do.

Yet at the grassroots worksite level, every agency in the study remained gendered in substantial ways. How to understand both questions – structure and change – is the subject of this chapter.

When Thorne went into Oceanside Elementary School and found that most of the teachers were women, she was not surprised. That is the usual arrangement in elementary schools in the United States, and most other rich countries. Similarly, Moodie was not astonished to find an all-male workforce at the Witwatersrand gold mines he investigated. That is the usual arrangement in South African mines, and in mining all over the world.

The gender regimes of these particular organizations, then, are part of wider patterns, which also endure over time. I call these wider patterns the *gender order* of a society. The gender regimes of institutions usually correspond to the overall gender order, but may depart from it. Change often starts in one sector of society and takes time to seep through into others.

When we look at a set of gender arrangements, whether the gender regime of an institution or the gender order of a whole society, we are basically looking at a set of *relationships* – ways that people, groups and organizations are connected and divided. 'Gender relations' are the relationships arising in and around the reproductive arena discussed in chapter 4.

It is important to notice that not all gender relations are direct interactions between women on one side and men on the other. The relations may be indirect – mediated, for instance, by a market, or by technologies such as TV or the Internet. Relationships among men, or among women, may still be gender relations – such as hierarchies of masculinity among men.

Gender relations are always being made and re-made in everyday life. If we don't bring it into being, gender does not exist. This point is forcibly made by ethnomethodology, a school of sociological research concerned with what we presuppose in everyday conduct. Candace West and Don Zimmerman, in a famous article called 'Doing gender' (1987), analyse the way in which gender is constituted in routine interaction. People engaging in everyday conduct – across the spectrum from conversation and housework to interaction styles and economic behaviour – are held accountable in terms of their presumed 'sex category' as man or woman. The conduct produced in the light of this accountability is not a product of gender, it is gender itself.

We make our own gender, but we are not free to make it however we like. Our gender practice is powerfully shaped by the gender order in which we find ourselves. That is what West and Zimmerman imply when they say we are 'held accountable' for our gendered conduct. Social theory has attempted to capture the fact of powerfully determined patterns in relationships with the concept of *structure*. Relations among people would have little significance if they were randomly arranged. Patterns in these relations would have little significance if they were ephemeral. It is the enduring or extensive patterns among social relations that social theory calls 'structures'. Thus we speak of class structures, kinship structures, age-grade structures, and so on.

The gender arrangements of a society constitute a social structure in this sense. For instance, if religious, political and conversational practices all place men in authority over women, we speak of a patriarchal structure of gender relations. Or if clans of men regularly marry each others' sisters, we speak of a kinship structure of exchange.

A structure of relations does not mechanically decide how people or groups act. That is the error of social determinism, and it is no more defensible than biological determinism. But a structure of relations certainly defines possibilities and consequences for action. In a strongly patriarchal gender order, women may be denied education and personal freedoms, while men may be cut off from emotional connections with children. In the gender order of contemporary Australia, Huey Brown (chapter 2) was given certain possibilities and not others; those he took up – such as drag, prostitution and domestic partnership – had major consequences for the rest of his life.

In this sense, social structure conditions practice. Yet structure does not exist in an abstract world that is somehow prior to everyday life. Social structures are brought into being by human behaviour, over time; they are historically constituted. Gender relations came into being, and keep on coming into being as we continue to engage in 'gendered modes of behavior', as Carol Hagemann-White (1987) puts it. Therefore, structure and change are not opposed; they are indeed part of the same dynamic of our social life.

Gender in four dimensions

When the pioneering British feminist Juliet Mitchell published *Woman's Estate* in 1971, she argued that women's oppression involves not one structure, but four: production, reproduction, socialization and sexuality.

Why make such distinctions? Many discussions of gender do not. For instance, the US feminist lawyer Catharine MacKinnon (1989) developed a theory of the state that treats 'gender hierarchy' as a homogeneous whole. The anthropologist Gayle Rubin (1975), in a very influential model of the 'sex/gender system', treated the whole field as a single system. But when we look closely into these theories, it becomes clear that each prioritizes a particular kind of relationship (MacKinnon: domination; Rubin: kinship). If we were to put power relations and kinship together in a more comprehensive picture of gender, we would need at least a two-dimensional model.

There are also practical reasons for acknowledging multiple dimensions in gender relations. We often experience disparities in gender relations, as if part of our lives were working on one gender logic, and another part on a different logic. When this happens in public life, not just in personal affairs, the complexity within the gender system becomes highly visible.

For instance, the modern liberal state defines men and women as citizens, that is, as alike. But the dominant sexual code defines men and women as opposites. Meanwhile, customary ideas about the division of labour in family life define women as housewives and carers of children. Accordingly, women entering the public domain – trying to exercise their rights as citizens – have an uphill battle to have their authority recognized. They may try to solve this problem by becoming honorary men, tougher than the toughest, like Margaret Thatcher in Britain and Condoleezza Rice in the United States. But most women in politics, like Hillary Clinton in the United States and Julia Gillard (deputy prime minister) in Australia, have to struggle for credibility; and Benazir Bhutto in Pakistan was murdered for her presumption.

There is, in my view, an overwhelming case for seeing gender relations as internally complex, i.e. as involving multiple structures. But how should we identify and map the structures involved?

Without much trouble, I can think of seven multi-level or multi-dimensional models of gender that different social scientists have developed to handle this problem, and doubtless there are more. Plainly, there is no unique solution: we can cut this cake in different ways.

Mitchell's original model mainly distinguished types of practice – work, child-rearing and sexuality – but mixed these with social functions, such as 'reproduction' and 'socialization'. The later models try, rather, to identify different social dynamics, forms of inequality or processes of change, and work back to their internal logics. Thus the British sociologist Sylvia Walby, in *Theorizing Patriarchy* (1990), distinguishes six structures in contemporary patriarchy: paid employment, household production, culture, sexuality, violence and the state. This greatly improves the account of patriarchy in MacKinnon's work; it is, however, still a model of inequality in gender relations. If we want also to theorize gender relations that are democratic, we need a different formulation.

The model I follow here distinguishes four dimensions of gender, and describes four main structures in the gender relations of contemporary industrial, post-industrial and global society. How far such a model can be applied in other times is an open question: it is a reasonable hypothesis that the structures of gender themselves change historically. In the rest of this section, I will discuss the meaning of these dimensions, and give some examples of the research about them.

Power relations: direct, discursive, colonizing

Power, as a dimension of gender, was central to the Women's Liberation concept of 'patriarchy': the idea of men as a dominant 'sex class', the analysis of rape as an assertion of men's power over women, and the critique of media images of women as passive, trivial and stupid. The power of husbands over wives and fathers over daughters is still an accepted idea in much of the world, even in modified forms such as the idea of the father as 'head of the household'. The continuing relevance of gendered power analysis is indicated by statistics of violence and abuse. For instance, the British Crime Survey of 2001, a large and carefully designed study of people's experience of crime, found that 21 per cent of British women, compared with 10 per cent of men, had experienced non-sexual force or threat at some time in their life; when it came to sexual victimization, 24 per cent of women, compared with 5 per cent of men, had experienced sexual violence (Walby and Allen 2004).

Women's Liberation recognized that patriarchal power was not just a matter of direct control of women by individual men, but was also realized impersonally through the state. A classic example, analysed in a famous article by MacKinnon (1983), is court procedure in rape cases. Independent of any personal bias of the judge, the procedures by which rape charges were tried at the time effectively placed the complainant rather than the defendant 'on trial'. The woman's sexual history, marital situation and motives in laying a charge were all under scrutiny.

Many attempts at legal reform have been made since. They have proved that the inbuilt biases in social assumptions and court procedure about sexual assault are very difficult to eliminate. It can still be a damaging experience for a woman to bring charges. In gender orders with oppressive controls over women's bodies, it can be positively dangerous. A scandal developed in 2007 about the case of a woman in Saudi Arabia who had been attacked and raped by a group of men; they were given light sentences, and *she* was sentenced to gaol and whipping for having been alone with a man to whom she was not related. When she appealed against the men's lenient sentences, her punishment was doubled. (Under international pressure, the Saudi government pardoned her.)

Another important case of the institutionalization of direct power relations is bureaucracies. Clare Burton (1987), an Australian social scientist who also served in public life as an equal opportunity commissioner, spoke of the 'mobilization of masculine bias' in selection and promotion of staff. By this she meant the impersonal but pervasive tendency, in organizations dominated by men, to favour criteria and procedures that favour men. Since men do control most large-scale organizations in the world (as noted in chapter 1), this is a far-reaching process producing gender inequality. Among them, of course, are armies – bureaucracies that specialize in violence. Men, rather than women, control the means of force in every part of the contemporary world.

Power also emerged as a major theme in Gay Liberation writing such as Dennis Altman's *Homosexual: Oppression and Liberation* (1972). Here the focus was on power applied to a specific group of men, through criminalization, police harassment, economic discrimination, violence and cultural pressure. Gay Liberation theorists linked the oppression of gay men with the oppression of lesbians and the oppression of women generally. This argument laid the foundation for the analysis of gendered power relations among men, and the distinction of hegemonic from subordinated masculinities, which is important in current research on men and masculinities (Connell and Messerschmidt 2005).

Another approach to power, popularized by the French historian Michel Foucault (1977), is sceptical of the idea that there is a unified agency of power in society. Rather, Foucault argued, power is widely dispersed, and operates intimately and diffusely. Especially it operates discursively, through the ways we talk and categorize people. It impacts directly on people's bodies as 'discipline', as well as on their identities, constituting subject positions that people take up. And it is productive, not just repressive: it generates forms of life.

This post-structuralist approach appealed to many feminist as well as gay theorists, who saw here a way of understanding the fine texture of power and its productiveness, the way power generates identities and practices. The discourse of fashion and beauty, for instance, positions women as consumers, subjects them to humiliating tests of acceptability, enforces arbitrary rules and is responsible for much unhappiness, ill health, and even some deaths by starvation in countries that have giant food surpluses (when girls' dieting turns into anorexia). Yet there is no man with a gun compelling women to do all this. As the 'lip gloss' in Barrie Thorne's ethnography illustrates, girls and young women enter the world of fashion and beauty because they want to, because it delivers pleasures. Taking up a subject position of desirable heterosexual femininity is both free choice and fiercely controlling.

The most sweeping exercise of power in the last 500 years, however, is not fully captured by either of these concepts. This is the creation of global empires, the invasion of indigenous land by the imperial powers – overseas mainly by Spain, Portugal, the Netherlands, France and Britain, overland by Russia and the United States – and the domination of the post-colonial world by economic and military superpowers.

As Valentine Mudimbe (1994: 140) says of the Congo, 'to establish itself, the new power was obliged to construct a new society'. Indigenous societies were pulverized, or mined for labour; and indigenous gender orders were transformed, by plantation economies, missions, population displacement and other processes. Colonizing forces, overwhelmingly men from the metropole, seized women's bodies as well as the land; and a fused gender/race hierarchy became a core feature of colonial society. It persists in the contemporary world.

Power is contested: even fascist dictatorships could not accomplish total domination. Gendered power is no more total than other kinds. Oppressive laws sparked campaigns for reform – such as the most famous of all feminist campaigns, the struggle for the vote. Domestic patriarchy may be weakened, or manoeuvred around, by the inhabitants of the 'red chamber' (as the classic Chinese novel put it), the women of the household. Discursive power can also be contested or transformed, as shown in the remarkable work of the Australian educator Bronwyn Davies. In *Shards of Glass* (1993), Davies shows how educators in the classroom can help children and youth gain control of gender discourses. Young people can learn how they are discursively positioned and regulated, and can learn to shift between, or manoeuvre among, identities.

Colonizing power was always contested, and women played an important part in colonial liberation struggles. Contemporary women's activism is found in every part of the world, and campaigns in different countries are increasingly connected (Moghadam 2005). As well as a concept of inequalities of power, then, we need a concept of equal power – of gender democracy.

Production, consumption and gendered accumulation

The 'sexual division of labour' was the first structure of gender to be recognized in social science, and remains the centre of most discussions of gender in anthropology and economics. In many societies, and in many situations, certain tasks are performed by men and others are performed by women. So, in the Aboriginal communities of the Australian central desert, hunting wallabies and kangaroos was undertaken by men, collecting root vegetables and seeds was mainly undertaken by women. In contemporary Europe and North America, computer software engineering is mainly done by men, while data entry is mainly done by women.

Such divisions of labour are common, perhaps even universal, through recorded history and across cultures. But while gender divisions of labour are common, there is not exactly the same division in different cultures or at different points of history. The same task may be 'women's work' in one context, and 'men's work' in another. Agricultural labour – digging and planting – is an important example.

A striking modern case is secretarial work. Being a clerk was originally a man's job – as described in Herman Melville's dark short story 'Bartleby the Scrivener' (1853). With the advent of the typewriter and the growing scale of office work, clerical work increasingly involved women. In the mid twentieth century it had became archetypical 'women's work', as Rosemary Pringle shows in *Secretaries Talk* (1989). But with the advent of the personal computer and word processing programs, 'the secretary' is disappearing as an occupational category. Clerical work is again, increasingly, being done by men – mixed in with other work, in new forms. A corporate executive nowadays may read and write sixty, eighty or a hundred e-mails a day.

In the industrial and commercial society that emerged in the global metropole a couple of hundred years ago, gender divisions between jobs are not the whole of the gender division of labour. We have to take account of the *total* social division of labour (Glucksmann 2000). There is a larger division between 'work', the realm of paid labour and production for markets, and 'home', the realm of unpaid labour. The whole economic sphere is culturally defined as a men's world (regardless of the presence of women in it), while domestic life is defined as a women's world (regardless of the presence of men in it).

The Norwegian sociologist Øystein Holter (2005) argues that this division is the structural basis of the modern Western gender order. It is what makes this system different from the gender orders of non-Western, non-capitalist societies. His point is not only that our notions of 'masculinity' and 'femininity' are closely connected with this division. Just as important, the social relations that govern work in these two spheres are different. In the economy, work is done for pay, labour is bought and sold, and the products of labour are placed on a market where profit prevails. In the home, work is done for love or mutual obligation, the products of labour are a gift, the logic of gift-exchange prevails. From these structural differences, Holter argues, flow characteristically different experiences for men and women – and our ideas about the different natures of men and women.

This is not exactly a distinction between 'production' and 'consumption', though that has been suggested by others as the economic core of the gender system. Domestic 'consumption' requires work, just as much as factory-based 'production' does. Housewives do not spend their time lolling on couches and scoffing chocolates. Housework and child care are hard work despite the advent of vacuum cleaners and microwave ovens. But housework and job-work are done in different social relations, as Holter correctly observes, and they consequently have very different cultural meanings.

The division of labour itself is only part of a larger pattern. In an industrial economy, the shared work of women and men is embodied in every major product, and every major service. Yet women and men are differently located in the economic process.

What can be seen here is a *gendered accumulation process*. Maria Mies (1986), the German theorist who has formulated this issue most clearly, suggests that the global economy developed through a dual process of colonization and 'housewifization'. Women in the colonized world, formerly full participants in local non-capitalist economies, have been increasingly pressed into the 'housewife' pattern of social isolation and dependence on a male breadwinner. Twenty years further on, the picture looks more complex, and there is more recognition of the significance of women's paid work, as a 'flexible', cheap labour force. Pamela Odih's *Gender and Work in Capitalist Economies* (2007) argues that the profitability of global manufacturing now crucially depends on women's labour in a global assembly line that is disaggregated, i.e. spread across regions.

Accumulation in the global economy is mainly organized through large corporations and global markets. The gender regimes of these institutions make it possible for them to apply the products of men's and women's joint work in gendered ways. The way firms distribute corporate income – through wage structures, benefits packages, etc. – tends to favour men, especially middle-class men. The products that corporations place on the market have gender effects and gendered uses, from cosmetics to cars to computers to machine guns.

The gendered accumulation process has many effects beyond the economy narrowly defined. For instance, where there is a gender division of labour in occupations – such as men being the majority in engineering and mechanical trades, women in arts-based and human service jobs – there will be a division in the education systems which prepare people for this work. It is not surprising to find that enrolments in high school and technical college courses in engineering studies and computer sciences are overwhelmingly boys, while enrolments in fine arts and hospitality are mainly girls. As Madeleine Arnot, Miriam David and Gaby Weiner (1999) show in a comprehensive study of gender in the British school system, difference in fields of study has survived despite historic changes that have closed the 'gender gap' in school retention.

Emotional relations

The importance of emotional attachment in human life was made clear 100 years ago in the work of Sigmund Freud. Borrowing ideas from neurology, but mainly learning from his own patients, Freud showed how charges of emotion – both positive and negative – were attached, in the unconscious mind, to images of other people. His famous analysis of the 'oedipus complex', the centrepiece of his theory of personality development, showed how important the patterning of these attachments, or cathexes, might be. (For careful definitions of these terms, see *The Language of Psycho-Analysis*: Laplanche and Pontalis 1973.)

Though he thought of his psychology as universal, Freud was theorizing the pattern of relationships inside a specific social institution, the bourgeois family in the society of the global metropole. His work thus opened up for investigation the social structuring of emotional relations, attachments or commitments.

Emotional commitments may be positive or negative, favourable or hostile towards the object. For instance, prejudice against women (misogyny), or against homosexuals (homophobia), is a definite emotional relationship. Emotional commitments are often, as Freud emphasized, both loving and hostile at once.

A major arena of emotional attachment is sexuality. Anthropological and historical studies have made it clear that sexual relations involve culturally formed bodily relationships, not a simple biological reflex (Caplan 1987). They have a definable social structure. Though sexuality cannot be reduced to gender, as Dowsett (2003) correctly argues in relation to the HIV/AIDS epidemic, sexuality is often organized on the basis of gender. The globally hegemonic pattern assumes cross-gender attraction; and makes a sharp distinction between cross-gender (heterosexual) and same-gender (homosexual) relations. In fact, this distinction is so important that it is commonly taken as defining different kinds of people ('homosexuals', 'heterosexuals'), and certain biologists go looking for a 'homosexual gene' to explain the deviance. (Curiously, no one has gone looking for the 'heterosexual gene'.)

But cross-cultural research shows that many societies do not make these distinctions, or do not make them in the same way. In classical Greece, the hegemonic pattern of sexuality and emotional commitment included strong relations among men, and between older men and male youth. More recently, the 'Sambia', a community in Papua New Guinea described in a well-known ethnography by Gilbert Herdt, *Guardians of the Flutes* (1981), treat same-gender sexuality as a ritual practice that all men are involved in at a particular stage of life. From a Western point of view, all Sambia men are homosexuals at one age, and all switch over to become heterosexuals at another. That is absurd, of course. From a Sambia point of view, they are simply following the normal development of masculinity.

In contemporary metropolitan society, households are expected to be formed on the basis of romantic love, that is, a strong individual attachment between two partners. This ideal is the basis of most television soaps and Hollywood weepies, and its importance is confirmed by research with groups who might be thought sceptical of it. They include the American university students in an ethnography by Dorothy Holland and Margaret Eisenhart, *Educated in Romance* (1990). As this ideal is spread around the world by religion, advertising and other cultural pressures, it comes into conflict with other ways of forming new households, especially arranged marriages that represent alliances between kinship groups. That conflict is a major source of tension between generations, and sometimes results in violence.

The other crucial emotional connection in the household is between parent and child, and this relationship too may be strongly gendered. In the globally hegemonic pattern, care and attachment to young children is the business of women, especially mothers; while fathers as breadwinners are expected to be emotionally distant. But this pattern is also under challenge, with 'new fatherhood' ideals spreading (see chapter 6). A study of the discourse of fatherhood in contemporary Japan by Taga Futoshi shows how difficult the emotional dilemmas can be. Whichever way fathers turn, the result can be conflict and a sense of guilt (Taga 2007).

Emotional relations are also found in the workplace. Arlie Hochschild's classic *The Managed Heart* (1983) analyses emotional labour in the US economy. There are many jobs where producing a particular emotional relationship with a customer is central to the work being done. These are, typically, gender-typed jobs. Hochschild's main examples are two jobs: airline hostess, in which workers are trained to produce sympathy and induce relaxation; and telephone debt collector, in which workers must display aggression and induce fear. Hochschild argues that this kind of labour is becoming more common with the expansion of service industries. If so, alienated relations based on commercialized feelings and gender stereotypes may be increasingly important in modern life.

Hostile emotional relationships are not only symbolic, like the ones enacted by Hochschild's debt collectors. Stephen Tomsen's (1998) study of homophobic killings in Australia, for instance, shows two major patterns of conduct. One is gang attacks in public places by young men who go looking for gender deviants to punish, a process that depends on mutual encouragement in the group. The other is killings by individuals in private. Some of these involve a violent response to a sexual approach (and perhaps to the killers' own desires) which they think calls their masculinity into question. Both patterns may result in killings of extreme brutality.

Symbolism, culture, discourse

All social practice involves interpreting the world. As post-structuralists observe, nothing human is 'outside' discourse. Society is unavoidably a world of meanings. At the same time, meanings bear the traces of the social processes by which they were made. Cultural systems bear particular social interests, and grow out of historically specific ways of life.

This point applies to gender meanings. Whenever we speak of 'a woman' or 'a man', we call into play a tremendous system of understandings, implications, overtones and allusions that have accumulated through our cultural history. The 'meanings' of these words are enormously greater than the biological categories of male and female. When the Papua New Guinea highland community studied by Marilyn Strathern (1978) say 'our clan is a clan of men', they do not mean that the clan entirely consists of males. When an American football coach yells at his losing team that they are 'a bunch of women', he does not mean that they can now get pregnant. But both are saying something meaningful, and, in their contexts, important.

The study of cultural representations of gender, of discursive constructions of gender, of gendered attitudes, value systems and related problems is probably the most active area of gender studies in the past two decades – in the rich countries of the global metropole. It is not so central in the developing world, where questions of power and material interest have higher priority. But even here it is relevant, as we see in Suparna Bhaskaran's *Made in India* (2004), a lively discussion of beauty pageants and the internationalization of Barbie-doll femininity, discrimination against homosexuals, and gender images in Indian media.

The best-known model of the structure of symbolism in gender derives from the French psychoanalyst Jacques Lacan. Lacan's analysis of the phallus as master-symbol gave rise to an interpretation of language as 'phallocentric', a system in which the place of authority, the privileged subjectivity, is always that of the masculine. The potentially infinite play of meaning in language is fixed by the phallic point of reference; culture itself embodies the 'law of the father'. If that is so, the only way to contest patriarchal meanings is to escape known forms of language. Hence feminist thinkers such as Xavière Gauthier (1981) developed an interest in women's writing as an oppositional practice that had to subvert the laws of culture.

Chris Weedon (1987) wonders how feminist theory could have adopted so deterministic a psychology, which gives no room for opposition, only for escape. Post-structuralism provided many tactics of escape, and queer theory's critique of 'heteronormativity' – of which, in a sense, Lacan had been the great theorist – leads to a strategy of cultural disruption. In current queer writing and politics, there is an energetic celebration of diversity in sexual identities and self-presentations, which takes pleasure in disruptions of familiar gender categories (e.g. Bauer, Hoenes and Woltersdorff 2007).

Though language – speech and writing – is the most analysed site of symbolic gender relations, it is not the only one. Gender symbolism also operates in dress, make-up, gesture, in photography and film, and in more impersonal forms of culture such as the built environment.

Rosa Linda Fregoso's *The Bronze Screen* (1993) illustrates some complexities of the cultural dynamics of gender in film. She studies films produced by Chicana/Chicano film-makers, about the community of Mexican affiliation in the south-western United States, outside the Anglo-centric Hollywood orbit. Chicano (men) film-makers, Fregoso observes, have not demeaned their women characters, but they have not given them an active role in discourse. Only with the advent of women film-makers did films start to explore generational difference, language, religion and relationships from women's standpoints, and show some of the tensions and ambiguities in Chicana women's social position and strategies.

Gender symbolism is constantly involved in social struggle. The complex politics of the anti-apartheid movement in South Africa show this, as different symbolic models of masculinity were put into play. One of the most formidable opponents of apartheid was the union movement, which constructed masculinity on a 'worker' model. A more ambiguous role was played by the Zulu-nationalist Inkatha movement, which tried to mobilize men around a 'warrior' image but stood for a conservative social order. And in the aftermath of the armed struggle, the 'young lions' of the African National Congress's guerrilla forces lost their social respect, and often fell into unemployment and violent crime (Waetjen 2004, Xaba 2001).

Symbolic expressions of gender change over time, and so do attitudes to gender equality. In an extended analysis of survey data from Germany and Japan, Ulrich Mohwald (2002) shows a shift of attitudes in both countries towards gender equality, though the course of events was different. The breadwinner/housewife model, formerly unknown in Japan, was constructed in the late nineteenth and early twentieth century CE as a middle-class ideal, and, following the Second World War, Japanese women endorsed both legal equality and this nuclear-family model. Another shift of opinion followed the Women's Liberation movement, with increasing value placed on women's careers and sharing work in the home. In Japan this shift occurred in the attitudes of all generations. In Germany, however, the recent shift away from traditional gender attitudes involves a generational split – it mainly happened in the younger generation.

Interweaving and intersection

The four dimensions just discussed are tools for thinking; they are not separate institutions. Though a division of labour is a different thing from a symbolic representation, no division of labour could long be sustained without symbolic categories. Birgit Pfau-Effinger's (1998) very sophisticated cross-national analysis of gender arrangements in European labour markets turns on this point – different cultural models of gender underpin different divisions of labour (and other aspects of the gender order). Similarly, the pattern of power displayed in rape trials is inseparably connected with stereotyped images of women's sexuality; mother/child and father/child emotional relationships are connected with the domestic division of labour and the wider economy. And so on. In a real-life context, the different dimensions of gender constantly interweave, and condition each other.

Further, the structures of gender are interwoven with other social structures. Fregoso's analysis of gender in Chicana/o film would make no sense if it were not seen in the context of ethnic inequality in US society. Hochschild's analysis of gendered emotional labour, like Pringle's analysis of secretarial work, presupposes a class structure, where groups of workers depend on capitalist corporations for their livelihood and have to deliver certain kinds of labour to get their wages.

This point has been emphasized in recent sociology under the heading of 'intersectionality'. It is an unfortunate term, because it suggests social structures are rigid arrangements that can be understood by a kind of geometry. Well, people do talk about 'social stratification', which is another spatial metaphor. But good analyses of intersectionality will think in terms of the mutual conditioning of structures – i.e. the ways they change each other – and how actual social situations are produced out of that mutual conditioning.

Ethnicity, for instance, is to a significant extent created through gender relations. The notion of an extended family is central to the rhetoric of ethnicity: 'our kith and kin' as the British used to say; 'brothers born of warrior stock', in the language of Zulu nationalism in South Africa (Waetjen and Maré 2001). Jill Vickers (1994) notes that male-dominated ethnic politics lays heavy emphasis on women's reproductive powers.

The idea that different structures of inequality shape each other is central to the analysis put forward by Helen Meekosha (2006). She observes that while gender theory has paid attention to intersections with race and class, it has paid little attention to disability. Meekosha notes that disability, too, is a matter of social relations – those that surround bodily impairments, in certain circumstances, but not others, turn impairments into disadvantages. Since gender fundamentally involves social embodiment (chapter 4), it must interact with social relations constituting disability. Meekosha examines the way this interaction occurs in settler-colonial societies such as Australia, and notes how colonization piled up disabling conditions for those indigenous people who survived the impact, and how conceptions of bodily superiority and inferiority were built into the ideology of race. But 'race' or ethnicity is a concept that requires gender – that calls into being a politics of populations, breeding, motherhood, masculine threat and defence. Conversely, gender impacts on the experience of disability:

> Yet the image of disability may be intensified by gender – for women a sense of intensified passivity and helplessness, for men a corrupted masculinity generated by enforced dependence. Moreover, these images have real consequences in terms of lack of access to education, employ-

ment, the nature of living arrangement and personal relationships, and the experience of victimization and abuse. (Meekosha 2006: 170)

For many purposes, we need to treat gender as a structure in its own right. We must avoid collapsing it into other categories, treating it as the effect of some other reality (as used to be done with class and is now sometimes done with discourse). But to have an adequate understanding of human life, we must also remember that gender relations always work in context, always interact with other dynamics in social life.

Gender as history

Ideologies of 'natural difference' have drawn much of their force from the traditional belief that gender never changes. Adam delved and Eve span, Men must work and Women must weep, Boys will be Boys. Serious analysis begins with the recognition that exactly the opposite is true: *everything about gender is historical.*

What does 'historical' mean? In the whole story of life on earth, human history represents a new process of change. Some time in the last 100,000 years, social dynamics replaced organic evolution as the central mechanism of change in our biosphere.

Some biological features of human ancestors were certainly preconditions of this change. The open architecture (to borrow a computer term) of the human hand, brain and speech apparatus makes an immense range of applications possible. The human body cannot scratch as sharply as a cat, dig as well as a wombat, swim as fast as a seal, manipulate as delicately as a monkey, or crush as powerfully as a bear. But it can do all these moderately well; and it can make tools to do them all *very* well. We are all cyborgs, in this sense. Yet the greatest human invention is other human beings. We not only create social relations, we teach new generations. With cumulating effects over time, social relations multiply the capacities of any individual body on the astonishing scale we see all around us.

In the broadest perspective, gender represents the transformation of sexual reproduction by social action. Human collective capacities, organized through social relations, lead to entirely new possibilities. Above this horizon is the history of gender: the course of events that has produced the actual gender orders we live in. The task of writing this history was defined in an influential article by the US historian Joan Scott, modestly called 'Gender: a useful category of historical analysis' (1986).

Can we identify a starting-point for this process? Since the nineteenth century, there has been endless speculation about the 'origins' of gender, primitive matriarchy or primordial patriarchy. As the French feminist Christine Delphy (1984) commented, most origin stories are not history but mythmaking, which serves to justify some political view in the present. Since she wrote, however, archaeological research has accumulated, and has begun to be combined with a social analysis of gender, in a way that offers the first serious evidence-based answer to this question.

The evidence is reviewed in 'Spear and digging stick: the origin of gender and its implications for the colonization of new continents' by the Australian archaeologists Jane Balme and Sandra Bowdler (2006), building on the work of other prehistorians. To summarize a complex argument: hunting large animals for meat, and collecting plant and small-animal food, appears as a gender division of labour in most known hunter–gatherer societies. This division does not follow biological capacities; both men and women are capable of doing both, so the gender division of labour is a social arrangement. It requires a complex communication system (presumably language), a social practice of sharing food in a continuing group, and also a cultural signification of gender, i.e. defining men and women as groups to whom different tasks can be allocated. Evidence for regular hunting and food sharing, for social symbolism and for the symbolic recognition of gender, all appear around the same period in the archaeological record, in camp sites, artefacts and rock paintings. They are associated, broadly, with the spread of anatomically modern humans (*Homo sapiens sapiens*) across Africa, Eurasia and Australia, probably 50,000 to 40,000 years ago.

The hypothesis is that a gender division of labour was an adaptation – a social not a genetic adaptation – to the spreading of human groups into unpredictable new environments where there was often a patchy food supply, and where a systematic combination of longer-distance hunting and local gathering was a highly effective solution. If this argument is correct, it identifies two of the four dimensions of gender discussed above – division of labour, and symbolism – as present in the formation of the earliest gender orders. It is interesting that power relations, i.e. matriarchy or patriarchy, are *not* implicated in this hypothesis.

Whatever account of the origins of the gender system we can give, its future history is not contained in a foundation moment. Rather, an open-ended social process is involved, which must be studied in all its complexity by patient examination of the historical records: the archaeological deposits, the written sources, the oral traditions.

Histories of this kind have flourished for several decades, being one of the main achievements of Women's Studies. It has produced superb work, such as *Family Fortunes* by Leonore Davidoff and Catherine Hall (1987), a social history of gender in the English middle class of the industrial revolution. On a larger scale, Pavla Miller's (1998) *Transformations of Patriarchy in the West, 1500–1900* traces a long historical shift in the pattern of gender relations, from household-based 'patriarchalism' in early modern Europe to a new organization of patriarchal power in industrial capitalism, privatized households and the bureaucratic state.

Recognizing the deeply historical character of gender has an important intellectual and political consequence. If a structure can come into existence, it can also go out of existence. The history of gender may have an end.

There are several ways in which gender relations might cease to be important conditions of social life. They might be weakened by an internal uncoupling, so that gender patterns in one domain of practice cease to reinforce those in another. For instance, symbolic gender distinctions might remain, but equality of power be achieved; or sexual connection cease to depend on membership of a gender group. Alternatively, gender relations might be overwhelmed by some other historical dynamic. This was expected by Marxists like Alexandra Kollontai (1977), who thought that proletarianization and socialist revolution would end the oppression of women. In our day, the total triumph of the market and complete individualization is often presented as the way to gender equality.

Finally, gender relations might be extinguished by a deliberate de-gendering, in which the reach of gender structure is reduced to zero. This logic is seen in equal opportunity and anti-discrimination reforms. Japanese reformers speak of 'gender-free' situations as the goal of reform. Not all feminists around the world agree with the de-gendering approach, and not all theorists assume that a complete de-gendering of society is possible. Nevertheless a gender-free society remains a useful conceptual benchmark for thinking about change.

Processes of change

Most discussions of why gender arrangements are changing have focused on external pressures: new technology, urban life, mass communications, secularism or just 'modernization'.

It is true that social forces such as these can produce change in gender relations. But gender relations also have internal tendencies towards change. Further, some of the 'external' pressures are themselves gendered from the start (for instance, the capitalist economic system). I think we have to consider gender always as a dynamic system – that is implied in seeing gender as historical – and in this section I will explore three of the dynamics.

Instability

Post-structuralist theory has recognized internal tendencies towards change by arguing that gender categories are inherently unstable. The uncertain and contested character of the category 'women' is a theme of Judith Butler's extremely influential book *Gender Trouble* (1990) and the feminist theorizing of Gayatri Chakravorty Spivak (1988). Gender identities are produced discursively. But meanings in discourse are not fixed. If we follow Derrida's analysis in *Of Grammatology* (1967), the founding text of postmodern philosophy, they are incapable of being fixed in any final way.

Further, there is no fixed connection between discursive identities and the bodies to which those identities refer. The signifier is able to float in a play of meanings and pleasures. That is sometimes thought to be a general feature of 'postmodern' life, and it certainly suggests that gender identities can be played with, taken up and abandoned, unpacked and recombined.

There are several difficulties with a concept of generalized instability. It can be made true by definition, but in that case is not interesting. If it is open to empirical checking, then it is difficult to avoid the fact that in some historical situations gender identities and relations change slowly, in other situations they change explosively. Sylvia Walby's *Gender Transformations* (1997) suggests that distinct 'rounds' of restructuring can be identified in the metropole. Nor does a concept of generalized instability give any grip on why some people would want to change gender arrangements, while others would resist. This is a question of central importance for the politics of gender. It raises the issue of the differing material interests that different groups have in an unequal society.

Finally, the idea of generalized instability of categories seems to have arisen in the global metropole, and perhaps captures something important about social life in the neoliberal rich countries of the contemporary world. In other parts of the world, however, the idea is perhaps less relevant. Gender boundaries seem to have hardened in some Arab countries and Iran in the last generation, for instance. Even Spivak is driven to the idea of 'strategic essentialism' when thinking about how to understand subaltern politics in India.

Contradiction

Thinking of gender as a social structure leads to another account of change. Structures develop *crisis tendencies*, that is, internal contradictions or tendencies that undermine current patterns, and force change in the structure itself. This approach to change is inspired by German critical theory, especially the work of Jürgen Habermas (1976), and feminist critiques that have spliced a gender dimension into critical theory (Johnson 1994).

A structural approach allows us to distinguish periods when pressures for change are well controlled, or are only gradually building, from periods when crisis tendencies erupt into actual crisis and force rapid change. It also allows us to identify interests that can be mobilized for and against change, by examining where different groups are located in the structure under pressure, and how they have been constituted within that structure.

Crisis tendencies can be identified in each of the four structures of gender relations defined earlier in this chapter. For reasons of space, I will describe only one of them here, the division of labour; but the approach will run through the discussion in the rest of the book.

The division of labour has been the site of massive change. Through the second half of the twentieth century CE, there was a world wide incorporation of women's labour into the market economy. The global labour force participation rate for women in 2007 was 52.5 per cent (compared with men's 78.8 per cent). In rich countries this took the form of growth in married women's workforce participation rates, i.e. movement from unpaid to paid work, especially in the service sector. In the developing world, the change took the form of an even more massive move into cities, into market-based agriculture and certain forms of industry.

There is an underlying contradiction between the roughly equal contribution to total social labour by women and men, and the gendered appropriation of the products of social labour. The gendered appropriation is seen in the unequal incomes of women and men as groups, the better conditions and career prospects that men generally (though not always) have, and the patriarchal inheritance of wealth and organizational control.

Women have a general interest in changing this. Hence women's activism in trade unions, in community organizing, and in pressure groups concerned with taxation and benefits. But the turbulence of the gendered accumulation process, and its intersection with class relations, create complexities. Economically privileged women (usually the most influential in politics), as well as men, have an interest in resisting economic reforms that would cut deeply into gender inequalities. This would deeply disturb the corporate system from which they benefit. So we do not see rich women on the picket lines supporting strikes at *maquiladora* dress factories or fast food outlets.

Crisis tendencies emerge on the small scale as well as the large; some examples in personal life will be seen in chapter 6. All four structures contain crisis tendencies but they are not the same tendencies; and as Sylvia Walby (1997) emphasizes, they do not develop at the same pace or mature at the same time. There is, inevitably, unevenness in the process of historical change. It is not surprising that gender orders are far from homogeneous, and that gender politics are complicated and turbulent.

Colonialism

The analysis of contradiction works best if there is a more or less coherent structure, an intelligible gender order, within which internal crisis tendencies can be said to arise. But what if the gender order has been smashed, the intelligibility of the world broken? That is precisely what happens in imperial conquest, with the arrival of the colonizing power discussed earlier.

And that is not something that happens just once, after which things return to normal. The continued existence of empire, the dynamism of the global metropole, the replacement of direct colonial power with post-colonial indirect power, the new structures of dominance in neoliberal globalization – all continue to seize and restructure the societies of the world periphery. A colonized society, as Georges Balandier (1955) argued in a penetrating analysis of change in central Africa, is a society in crisis.

Here the 'intersectionality' argument seems to reach its most powerful form, with gender restructured by imperialism. But imperialism is itself a deeply gendered system, from the moment of colonial conquest by a workforce of men (soldiers, sailors, administrators, priests) to the stabilization of colonial societies with their racial hierarchies and institutions of plantation labour and domestic service. The creation of new masculinities occurs among both colonizers and colonized, as Ashis Nandy (1983) pointed out. Historians have traced the construction of gendered institutions on the colonial frontier. Robert Morrell's *From Boys to Gentlemen* (2001a), for instance, documents the creation of a system of elite boys' schools in the British colony of Natal, intended to produce a form of masculinity capable of ruling a subject population; and also the creation of a network of gendered institutions, such as volunteer regiments and local associations through which the ruling was done.

Neoliberal globalization similarly restructures local gender orders, as well as being itself a deeply gendered process (as will be seen in chapter 7). A good deal of evidence about this is emerging in recent research on motherhood. Let me give an illustration from central America. In Nicaragua, following the election of a right-wing government led by Violeta Chamorro in 1990, a neoliberal package was introduced involving public sector cuts, privatization of state agencies and reduced social services. Julie Cupples' (2005) interviews with single mothers in the town of Matagalpa show these changes reflected in mothers' loss of dignity and greater difficulty in making ends meet. But the women of Matagalpa responded actively. With the growth of an informal economy with improvised money-making activities, the women moved into employment, however precarious, more confidently than the men – often reducing or abandoning their housework commitments to do so. Having to care for children obliged the women to generate a family income. Over time, Cupples suggests, paid work has become consolidated as part of women's identity; being a breadwinner became part of motherhood, rather than being opposed to it. In nearby El Salvador a similar neoliberal settlement emerged after a compromise between a right-wing US backed government and an armed resistance movement. Irina Carlota Silber's (2004) ethnographic observations show women there have to deal with a high level of gendered violence, as well as making a precarious living, in the aftermath.

The outcome of such processes is not a fixed gender order. It is, rather, a reconfigured terrain on which new processes of change and new social struggles arise. This is dramatically shown in the reshaping of gender relations in post-apartheid South Africa, where rival patriarchies, and movements of gender reform among men as well as women, are in contestation (Morrell 2001b).

This is only a beginning with the task of understanding change in gender relations on a world scale. I will return to the issue in the next two chapters; it is one of the most active, and also most difficult, areas of gender research today.

6

Gender in personal life

To most people, being a man or a woman is above all a matter of personal experience. It is something involved in the way we grow up, the way we conduct family life and sexual relationships, the way we present ourselves in everyday situations, and the way we see ourselves. In this chapter I examine issues that arise in this realm of intimacy, and reflect on how to understand what happens here.

Growing up gendered: sex role socialization, psychoanalysis and embodied learning

When sex role theory provided the main framework, there was a fairly straightforward account of how people acquired gender. Babies were, from the start, identified as either female or male and put in pink and blue baby clothes respectively. Blue babies were expected to behave differently from pink babies – rougher and tougher, more demanding and vigorous. In time they were given toy guns, footballs and construction sets. The pink babies, by contrast, were expected to be more passive and compliant, also prettier. As they grew older they were dressed in frilly clothes, given dolls and make-up kits, told to take care of their appearance and be polite and agreeable.

In the fullness of time, the former blue babies would be taught to run cars and solve mathematical equations, to compete in the marketplace and earn a living, and to pursue former pink babies. The former pink babies would be taught to cook, to be good at human relations, to do what they were told, and to make themselves attractive to the former blue babies.

Put more formally, the idea was that sex roles were acquired by socialization. Various 'agencies of socialization', notably the family, the school, the peer group and the mass media, took the growing child in hand. Through an immense number of small interactions, these agencies conveyed to the girl or the boy the social 'norms' or expectations for behaviour. This could be done by imitating admired 'role models', such as a father might be for a boy; or it could be done piecemeal. Compliance with the norms would lead to rewards, or 'positive sanctions': smiles from mother, approval from friends, good marks at school, success in the dating game, appointment to a good job. Nonconformity or deviance would lead to negative sanctions, all the way from frowns and cross voices to getting beaten up or sent to gaol.

With this mixture of positive and negative reinforcement, most children would learn the gender-appropriate behaviour as they grew up. They would eventually do it automatically, and come to think of themselves as the kind of people they were supposed to be. They would actually develop the traits of character the society thought appropriate for women or for men, and thus 'internalize' the norms. As fully socialized members of society, they would in turn apply negative sanctions to deviants, and convey the norms to the next generation. The sex role system thus seemed to have an inbuilt stabilizing mechanism, and would reproduce itself over time. Of course the process could go wrong, for instance if fathers disappeared from families and boys lacked role models, which would probably lead to juvenile delinquency.

There is something to be said for this story of how gender is acquired, but there are also severe problems with it; so severe, in fact, that the socialization model should be abandoned.

First, it is far too monolithic. In principle, a different sex-role-socialization story could be told for every culture in the world, assuming they all have different norms, and this is sometimes how the issue is treated in elementary textbooks. But the world does not consist of a mosaic of neatly distinct cultures. Cultures were smashed, fragmented and re-composed by conquest, colonization, migration and contemporary globalization. The ethnic pluralism of modern societies (e.g. different traditions about wife/husband relations among Chinese-Americans, African-Americans and Anglo-Americans, or between Turkish immigrants and native-born Germans) involves hierarchies of resources and respect, often enforced by violence. The model of sex role socialization mistakes what is dominant for what is normative. Further, multiple patterns arise within gender relations, through the contradictions and dynamics discussed in chapter 5. There are always multiple patterns of masculinity and femininity to complicate the picture of learning.

Second, the socialization model supposes that learning gender is a matter of acquiring *traits*, that is, regularities of character that will produce regularities of behaviour. Sex role theory, basically, is a version of the difference model of gender discussed in chapter 4. But, as the research reviewed in chapter 4 shows, major differences in traits between women and men (also girls and boys) are hard to detect. Even when the scales used by psychologists detect some average differences between women and men, they are slight in comparison with the variation among women, and among men. It is clear that growing up gendered cannot be just a matter of internalizing role norms.

Third, the socialization model pictures the learner as passive, while the agencies of socialization are active. When we turn to real situations where gender learning is going on, they do not look much like this. Consider the American elementary schools studied by Barrie Thorne (chapter 2). The boys and girls here are not lying back and letting the gender norms wash over them. They are constantly active in the matter. They take up gender divisions supplied by adults, sometimes accept them, and sometimes don't. They set up their own gender divisions in the playground, and then disrupt them. They try out gendered self-presentations (e.g. the older girls putting on lip gloss), and some of them try cross-gender presentations (e.g. girls being sporty or rough). They complain, joke, fantasize and question about gender matters. Similar energy and activity appear in other studies of gender learning, such as the British upper secondary students described by Máirtín Mac an Ghaill in *The Making of Men* (1994).

The socialization model seems to miss the *pleasure* which is obvious in much gender learning, the enthusiasm with which young people take up gender symbolism (e.g. sexy clothes) and construct gendered relations (e.g. teenage dating). Nor does it give much insight into the *resistance* which many young people put up to hegemonic definitions of gender: the boys who hate sport, the girls who want to be astronauts, the teen-agers who recognize themselves as gay. It also seems to miss the *difficulty* which is involved in constructing identities and working out patterns of conduct in a gender order marked by power, violence and alienated sexualities.

Let me give two examples from research with young people. Sue Lees' disturbing study of fifteen- and sixteen-year-old girls in Britain, *Losing Out* (1986), showed almost intolerable dilemmas about sexual reputation in dealing with boys who share a misogynist culture. As one girl remarked: 'It's a vicious circle. If you don't like them, then they'll call you a tight bitch. If you go with them they'll call you a slag afterwards.'

Ann Ferguson's study of *Bad Boys* (2000), children at an elementary school in California who are sent to the 'punishing room', finds that the children 'at risk' of disciplinary action are mostly African-American boys. Ferguson interviewed the parents and the children as well as school personnel, including an amazing interview with one mother, Mariana, who had been arrested for whipping a child. The research showed how breaking rules and resisting learning could become a means of constructing masculinity, as early as elementary school, in a situation of disempowerment and racial labelling; and how difficult were the dilemmas faced by parents too, aware of the pressures and risks that would be faced by Black boys when they had grown up.

The fourth problem with the socialization model is that it recognizes just one direction of learning – towards the sex role norms. It is difficult, in such a framework, to understand the changes of direction that often appear in a young person's life, coming apparently from nowhere. Developmental crises sometimes occur, with a sudden change in gender practice. There can be a shift of attachment from mother to father, a new level of aggression, a sudden burst of sexual activity, a turning away from girls or boys. Rather than just failing to 'internalize' the gender patterns of her/his parents, a young person may vehemently reject them, criticize their political or human inadequacy, and launch out on a search for something different.

I have spent so much time on the weaknesses of the sex-role-socialization model for two reasons. First, it is still the most popular view of gender learning, and therefore the most popular alternative to the body-machine, essentialist ideas of gender discussed in chapter 4. Second, the research that shows its difficulties also points to better ways of understanding gender formation.

The contradictory character of human development is much better understood by psychoanalysis, though psychoanalysis is currently much less influential in social science. Freud's case studies – Dora, Little Hans and the 'Wolf Man' are the most famous – emphasize conflict and contradiction. Freud recognized that a person is often developing in different directions at the same time, at unconscious and conscious levels. Psychoanalysis has been developing for a century and contemporary schools remain deeply divided, but, in virtually all of them, this insight seems important.

In Freud's account, gender development centred on the oedipus complex – the emotional crisis of middle childhood in which the child's sexual desire, focused for the moment on mother and father, was repressed. This crisis set up an unconscious pattern of motivation, different for boys and girls, that continued to influence their mental life from the shadows, and in the normal case led to adult heterosexual attraction. Psychoanalysis thus offered an explanation of how a conventional gender pattern was transmitted from generation to generation with apparent ease, shaping the very desires of adult men and women. But it also showed that this effect was achieved through emotional contradictions and crises which could be resolved along other paths. Thus non-normative gender development could also be understood.

Psychoanalytic theories and methods have always been controversial. There is a strong tendency for psychoanalytic movements to turn into cult-like celebrations of a founding father (Freud, Jung, Adler, Lacan and, for some of the smaller sects, a founding mother such as Klein), which makes the whole thing difficult to take seriously. Yet there are powerful insights here, about the contradictory character of development, about the importance of bodily desire and about unconscious motivation. If we take psychoanalysis as opening up issues about human development that are hard to see from other perspectives, it should be counted an important tool for gender analysis.

A decent account of how we acquire gender must recognize both the contradictions of development, and the fact that learners are active, not passive. People growing up in a gendered society unavoidably encounter gender relations, and actively participate in them. This participation is disorganized to some extent, because the patterns of their lives are not yet settled. Hence the element of anarchy in 'gender play', as Thorne describes it, with children dodging in and out of gender patterns. This anarchy can reappear later in life if there is an attempt to unlearn or re-learn gender patterns, where it may be experienced as more terrifying – gender vertigo rather than gender play.

Chapter 4 argued that we must recognize the agency of bodies in the social world. The active learner is embodied. The pleasure involved in learning gender is to some extent a bodily pleasure, pleasure in the body's appearance and in the body's performance. Bodily changes such as menarche, first ejaculation, the 'breaking' of a boy's voice and the development of a girl's breasts are often important in the development of gender. Their meanings are nevertheless ambiguous until they are given definition by the society's gender symbolism.

Because gender practice involves bodies but is not biologically determined, the gender practice being learned may actually be hostile to bodies' physical well-being. Young men in rich countries such as the United States and Australia, enacting their fresh-minted masculinities on the roads, die in appalling numbers in traffic accidents, at a rate four times higher than young women. A large number of adolescent girls and young women go in for dieting, in an attempt to maintain their heterosexual attractiveness, and for a certain percentage this escalates into life-threatening anorexia. In poorer countries, the circumstances are different but the stakes are also very high. For instance, in the Palestinian confrontation with Israeli occupation, the *intifada*, most of the direct resistance has been carried out by very young men and boys. As Julie Peteet (1994) shows in a terrifying ethnography, being beaten or arrested by the Israeli army and police became a kind of rite of passage into masculinity for Palestinian youth, and, of course, some of them were killed.

Embodied learners encounter the gender regimes of the institutions they come in contact with. The socialization model was right about the importance of the family, the school and the media in children's lives, but failed to recognize the internal complexity of these institutions. Conflicting models and messages abound. In a school, the teachers present a range of different patterns of masculinity and femininity to the children, simply as a result of the diversity in their own lives. The children are likely to pick up some of the gender politics among their elders. For instance Australian boys learn to insult each other as 'poofters' (fags). Their elders, in turn, may be divided about gender issues in their treatment of the children. Even in a two-parent family, there is room for argument about how to bring up a girl or a boy.

To add to complexity, the same experience may be interpreted in different ways. For instance a boy growing up in a situation of domestic violence, where his father often bashes his mother, may incorporate violence towards women into his own repertoire of masculinity. Many do. But the boy may also react against it out of terror, or may side with his mother and reach for a totally different relationship with women in his own life. Some time ago Carol Hagemann-White (1992), reviewing German experience, noted that intimate violence has a deep connection with the overall gender hierarchies in society. She argued, and it is now widely accepted, that, though work with perpetrators is difficult, and the driving force for change comes from women, campaigns to prevent gender violence necessarily involve action by groups of men and male youth. Radhika Chopra's *Reframing Masculinities* (2007), from which one of the cases in chapter 2 was taken, shows how this logic is currently at work in India.

Institutions do not mechanically determine young people's learning. But they do shape the consequences of what young people do – the risks they run, the recognition they get, the networks they gain access to, the penalties they pay. For instance adopting a resistant pattern of masculinity may point a boy out of the school system, as Ferguson's study shows. On the other hand, there are patterns of masculinity, more familiar in elite schools, which are equally competitive but pursue competition through the channels provided by the school.

The diversity of gender patterns among children and youth show up with particular clarity in research that looks across different social

groups. Stephen Frosh, Ann Phoenix and Rob Pattman, in a very perceptive study called *Young Masculinities* (2002), report on eleven- to
fourteen-year old boys in twelve secondary schools across London. They
show that ethnic position is prominent in London boys' views about
masculinity – Afro-Caribbean boys being thought high in masculinity
and Asian boys low; and that relations with the schools are ambivalent,
academic success being both desired and thought feminine. Above all,
the study shows that diversity in the boys' lives exists in tension with
'canonical narratives' of masculinity, i.e. a hegemonic pattern (an admired
physical toughness, sports skills, heterosexuality), which all boys
acknowledge but most do not fully inhabit. Rather, their adolescence is
marked by a complex negotiation with the hegemonic definition of
gender, in which they may criticize some versions of masculinity as *too*
tough, while rejecting others as effeminate.

When children and youth grapple with their places in a gendered
world, they are not, for the most part, internalizing gender-specific
behaviours. (Such behaviours are rare, as I noted in chapter 4.) Children
are, much more importantly, learning how gender relations work, and
how to navigate among them.

Much of young people's learning about gender is learning what we
might call *gender competence*. Young people learn how to negotiate the
gender order. They learn how to adopt a certain gender identity and
produce a certain gender performance – how to 'do gender', as West and
Zimmerman (1987) famously put it. Young people also learn how to
distance themselves from a given gender identity, how to joke about their
own performance. Most boys and girls fail to match gender ideals – ideals
of handsomeness, beauty, skill, achievement or recognition. But most of
them cope.

It is helpful to think of active learning as involving a commitment of
oneself in a particular direction. The learner does not simply absorb what
is to be learnt; the learner engages with it, moves forward in life in a
particular direction. The pleasure in gender learning, already mentioned,
is the pleasure of creativity and movement. Gender learning can occur
at any moment that a young person encounters gender relations in the
situations of everyday life, and grapples with those situations. It is not
usually planned, and it need not be explicitly named as gender – it may
be thought of as 'sports I enjoy', 'fights with my parents', 'jobs I am
suited for', in early life, and then 'being a parent', 'holding a job', etc.,
in later life. A lovely piece of research that shows this lifelong process is
Wendy Luttrell's *Schoolsmart and Motherwise* (1997), based on interviews with African-American and White working-class women in adult
education programmes in the United States, looking back down the years
of their lives.

From such a perspective it is clear that gender learning takes definite shapes. From early in the process, what is learnt is connected with other pieces of learning. Children learn about, and create in their own lives, patterns of practice – the *configurations* of gender practice in personal life that we call 'femininity' and 'masculinity'.

Gender configurations, being patterns of activity, are not static. (This is one reason why the attempts by some psychologists to capture masculinity and femininity with standardized paper-and-pencil scales do not work very well.) The process of engaging with a situation, moving forward, happens not just at the level of particular pieces of learning, it also happens on the larger scale of a whole life. Masculinity and femininity are 'projects', to use a term suggested by the philosopher Jean-Paul Sartre (1968). They are patterns of a life-course projected from the present into the future, bringing new conditions or events into existence which were not there before. Simone de Beauvoir's *The Second Sex* (1949) includes a long section that discusses alternative life projects for women as they existed in European society and history.

Seeing gender learning as the creation of gender projects makes it possible to acknowledge both the agency of the learner and the intractability of gender structures. Gender patterns develop in personal life as a series of encounters with the constraints and possibilities of the existing gender order. In these encounters the learner improvises, copies, creates, and thus develops characteristic strategies for handling situations in which gender relations are present – learns how to 'do gender' in particular ways. Over time, especially if the strategies are successful, they crystallize into recognizable patterns of femininity or masculinity.

The existing structures of the gender order mean that some strategies are more likely than others to get results. So there is likely to be overlap in the gender projects, a degree of social standardization of individual lives. We might call these common *trajectories* of gender formation. They are what researchers pick up as patterns of 'masculinity' or 'femininity' in life-history and ethnographic research.

Gender projects are not one-dimensional or smooth, and may involve heavy costs. A classic example is given in the Nigerian novelist Chinua Achebe's very famous story *Things Fall Apart* (1958). The hero has a life project of upward mobility, gaining respect in his village and district by enactment of an exemplary masculinity. He is a successful farmer, husband and father. But this requires him to reject the erring wife with whom he is, in fact, deeply in love. The resulting tension begins the disintegration which, by the end of the story, with the arrival of missionaries and colonial power, becomes catastrophic.

For psychology, the classic example of gender contradiction in development is the 'oedipus complex' identified by Freud in middle childhood.

In the mainstream psychoanalytic view, which centres on the boy, the child's active desire for the mother eventually meets an overwhelming prohibition created by the father's power (and behind that, the codes of society). The resulting psychological crisis drives the desire underground – more technically, creates a system of repressions out of which adult personality is formed. Freud always had difficulty adapting this model for girls.

In the more-or-less normal case, the oedipal crisis does get resolved and the child moves on to a new stage of development; when it does not, the sufferer may end up on the psychoanalyst's couch. We need not agree with Freud's specific account of the oedipus complex to agree with the broader argument. A life-history, and a gender project within a life-history, does not unfold seamlessly. It involves a number of distinct *moments* in which different gender commitments are made, different strategies are adopted, or different resolutions of gender issues are achieved.

Let me give as an example my own research with a small group of men in the early days of the Australian 'green' movement (Connell 1995: ch. 5). Most of them grew up in homes with a conventional gender division of labour, and in childhood and adolescence began to make a commitment to hegemonic masculinity. But this moment of engagement was followed by a moment of negation, as they began to distance themselves from hegemonic masculinity, for a variety of reasons, including family conflict. Most then, in the counter-culture or in the green movement, encountered feminism and were obliged to confront gender issues head-on: this was a moment of separation from hegemonic masculinity. Some were still at this point when we interviewed them. Some, however, had moved on to a moment of contestation, starting a political project of reforming masculinity and committing themselves to gender equality.

I do not believe there is a standard set of stages in gender formation – though a number of psychologists, from Freud on, have thought there is. What we know about the diversity of gender orders makes it unlikely that there are universal rules for the way gender is learnt. Perhaps the nearest thing to a universal rule is the fact of qualitative change. Any particular gender project, for an individual or a group in their distinct historical setting, is likely to involve points of transition, different moments of development.

The diversity of masculinities and femininities shown by a great deal of gender research implies different trajectories of gender formation. Class inequalities, ethnic diversity, regional difference, national origin and migration create different experiences of childhood. Further, major social changes may alter relations between parents and children.

The collapse of the Soviet Union and the formation of a new capitalism in the 1990s involved the most dramatic economic decline in recent world history. Jakob Rigi's (2003) heartbreaking ethnography traces the consequences in Kazakhstan. As in other post-Soviet republics, a few families seized control of most public assets, and the majority were thrown into poverty and insecurity. This drove a wedge between working-class parents and children. The parents, for the most part, held to the Soviet-era values of education and the work ethic. Youth, who had already in the late Soviet period been moving towards Western consumerism, saw that the old strategies no longer worked, and in an environment of disillusion, casual employment and family quarrels, carved out new paths for themselves, which were often sharply gendered. Young men moved into crime or security work (or both), young women into prostitution or jobs where they could trade on their sexuality – a massive commodification of sexuality and collapse of women's rights being a feature of the famous 'transition to democracy'. Meanwhile rich parents could buy both consumer goods and education for their children and find them good jobs in the new economy.

The diversity of trajectories is also shown in a British study, Gillian Dunne's *Lesbian Lifestyles* (1997). Some of the women she interviewed served an 'apprenticeship' to conventional femininity, some were tomboys; some grew up in families with a conventional division of labour, some in egalitarian homes. Dunne emphasizes the agency of the girls in responding to these experiences. But she also notes the intractability of the gender order. As they moved into adolescence, where the 'romance' and 'dating' culture ruled, many of the girls found the middle ground in gender relations, which they had previously occupied, disappearing beneath their feet. As one woman, Connie, recalls:

> The whole thing changed, suddenly they became totally different people. I thought what is this thing that happens to everyone else and doesn't happen to me? . . . I didn't know how to behave, quite honestly. They all seemed to have this secret code that they all learned, and I didn't. They all knew how to behave at discos, and I would sit pinned to the wall terrified. Where did they learn this? I didn't have it. It was some sort of pattern of social behaviour that everyone fell into, and I didn't have it – God! . . . The big 'goo goo' eyes came out, the painted faces, and the frocks, and all that stuff, and the act, the peacock act, basically attracting.

Diversity does not mean chaos. Children deal with the same institutions and with overlapping groups of adults. One of the key competencies children learn is to recognize the prevailing masculinities and femininities in the adult world. Whatever ideology prevails in the gender order, children grow up under its shadow.

It is difficult to make a complete break with the gender customs one has grown up with. With this in mind, Gay Liberation activists spoke of 'self-oppression' among gay men. A heterosexual version of the same dilemma is presented in Doris Lessing's famous novel *The Golden Notebook* (1962). Lessing pictures her heroines Anna and Molly as trying to conduct independent lives as 'free women', consistent with the principles of British left-wing politics. But they find their autonomy constantly undermined by their emotional need for relationship with a man. Their political experience, even their financial independence, makes no difference.

Yet the gender order does change, and this makes possible new personal trajectories, new paths of learning. Young women growing up after the Women's Liberation movement have their own dilemmas about jobs, marriage and children, as can be seen in the stories told in Chilla Bulbeck's three-generation study, *Living Feminism* (1997). But they do not face the same impasse as women of Doris Lessing's generation.

Belief in gender equality has also spread among younger men, in some places. Witness the national study of men in Germany by Zulehner and Volz (1998), where men below fifty endorse a gender-equal model of family life, and reject 'traditional' norms, much more often than men above fifty. However this does not seem to be universal. Lineke Stobbe's (2005) study of gender talk among factory workers in Argentina finds both women and men accepting a consensus ideology in which admired men are in charge, breadwinners, virile and gallant towards women; while women – although working in a factory – are still responsible for children and are regarded as weaker and more vulnerable. To understand the forces shaping paths of gender development, we have to move outward from personal life to larger arenas. This will be the subject of chapter 7.

Gender identity

Perhaps the commonest way of understanding the presence of gender in personal life is through the concept of 'gender identity'. The term 'identity' has a long history in philosophy and literature, and has gone through a curious shift in meaning. It was originally one of a family of philosophical and religious terms that expressed the theme of unity. By the nineteenth century the term had become thoroughly naturalized in English and was used in literature as well as philosophy and mathematics. It was still generally used with the meaning of 'sameness', though sometimes in the sense of personal existence, or to emphasize who I am as against who I am not.

By the late nineteenth century, however, 'who I am' had become a problem for the speakers of European languages. The feudal social order was dead, replaced by a restless capitalism, gigantic new cities, enormous labour migrations and turbulent working classes. At the same time, global empires brought Europeans and North Americans face to face with radically different cultures, and urgently posed the question of human sameness and difference.

Western bourgeois culture – now the dominant culture in the world – came to include a powerful ideology of innate differences between people. These were supposed to be differences of character as well as physical type, and were reflected in the hierarchies of class, race and gender. Yet this belief was under challenge as soon as it was formulated. It was challenged by anti-colonial intellectuals such as Mohandas Gandhi, who argued against the idea of inherited or acquired superiority on the grounds that 'all have the same soul'.

Belief in fixed differences was challenged in another way by the radical psychology of Sigmund Freud and his followers. Psychoanalytic insights became the basis of the twentieth century's most influential statement about identity. Erik Erikson's famous *Childhood and Society* (1950) interpreted a range of modern personal, social and political problems as difficulties in achieving identity: 'The study of identity, then, becomes as strategic in our time as the study of sexuality was in Freud's time' (1950: 242). But where Freud had focused on conflicts involving unconscious agencies of the mind (the 'id' and the 'superego'), Erikson emphasized the conscious agency, the 'ego'. The ego is the mental agency involved in transactions with the outside world, the agency where the conscious sense of self is located. To Erikson the term 'identity' meant the coherence of the psychological mechanisms by which the ego handles the pressures that impinge on it – from the unconscious mind, on the one side, and the outside world, on the other. The question 'who am I?' is, in principle, answered by the ego's success in mastering the trials and tribulations of psychological development. This was, Erikson thought, a particularly important issue in adolescence.

The key application of this concept to gender was made by the American psychiatrist Robert Stoller (1968), who altered it in two ways. First, the 'core gender identity' that Stoller saw as the basis of adult personality was supposed to be formed very early in life, not in adolescence. Second, the concept of identity acquired a different frame of reference. Erikson referred to the integration of the ego as a whole. Stoller's conception was much more specific. To talk of 'gender identity' is to talk only of *one aspect* of the person – her or his involvement in gender relations or sexual practice.

To Stoller this narrower focus did not matter because he assumed that the integration of the personality as a whole *was* largely focused on the sense of being a male or a female. But on any other view of personality and social process, an exclusive focus on gender is a problem. We can speak just as meaningfully of 'racial identity', 'generational identity' or 'class identity'. If we acknowledge the 'constant interweaving' (Bottomley 1992) of these social relations, which is now common in discussions of 'intersectionality', we *must* attend to these other forms of identity in order to understand gender identity. The concept of 'identity' formulated by Stoller thus leads towards a conception of identity as inherently plural rather than unitary.

A model of identity built on gender dichotomy was more easily accepted by the 1970s because American feminist research emphasized gender difference in the rearing of children. The most influential statement was Nancy Chodorow's *The Reproduction of Mothering* (1978). Chodorow's argument linked the gender division of labour, which assigned the task of caring for babies and infants exclusively to women, with the paths of development for girls and boys that resulted from their different emotional situations in early childhood. Girls, brought up by a parent of their own gender, tend to have less distinct ego boundaries. When they grow up they have a stronger motivation for nurturing children. Boys, pushed towards separation from a mother responding to the gender distinction, tend to have an earlier discontinuity or break in development. They have more difficulty in establishing gender identity, and stronger boundaries to the self in adulthood.

Though it has been well established that men *can* 'mother' (Risman 1986), it is still the case that, in contemporary Western society, few of them do. But the reasons for this may be economic rather than psychological. Introducing paid leave for fathers of young children, in Scandinavia, has been a successful reform (Holter 2003). There has also been more recognition – by Chodorow (1994) among others – that we do not find dichotomous gender patterns in adult personalities. That of course was a major conclusion of the 'sex similarity' research discussed in chapter 4.

Variation within gender categories is plain in the recent research on masculinity. In contrast to the way '*the* male role' was discussed in the 1970s, it has become common to speak of 'masculinities' in the plural. There is considerable diversity between societies in their constructions of gender for men. This can readily be seen by comparing descriptions of masculinities in Latin America, the Middle East, southern Africa and east Asia (Gutmann 2001, Ghoussoub and Sinclair-Webb 2000, Morrell

2001). There is also considerable evidence that there are multiple masculinities within the same society, even within the same institution, peer group or workplace. A striking example is Douglas Foley's (1990) ethnography of a high school in a Texas country town in the United States. Here the interplay of gender, class and ethnicity constructs several versions of masculinity. There is the dominant group of Anglo 'jocks', antiauthoritarian Mexican-American 'vatos', and the group which Foley calls ironically the 'silent majority'.

The trend has therefore been to speak of multiple gender and sexual identities. Some psychologists, for instance, have mapped out the stages of acquisition of a 'homosexual identity' (Troiden 1989) as one among a number of possible sexual identities in modern society. But there is a significant shift of ground in moving from the concept of 'identity' to the concept of 'gender identity' or 'sexual identity'. With the categories seeming more and more complex, the concept of identity has increasingly been used for claims made by individuals about who or what they are in terms of *difference* from other people.

This is closely related to the growth, especially in the United States, of 'identity politics'. One becomes a member of a social movement by claiming the identity (as Black, as a woman, as lesbian, etc.) that the movement represents. Queer politics takes the process a step further. Queer activists have challenged taken-for-granted communities by emphasizing their diversity: highlighting the presence of Black lesbians in White-dominated lesbian communities, for instance. At the extreme, the concept of identity becomes a way of naming one's uniqueness.

Even the identities on which social movements have been based prove, on close examination, to be less solid than we might think. Arne Nilsson's (1998) beautifully crafted study of homosexual history in the Swedish city of Göteborg identifies three ways of being homosexual: 'so', commonly a bit effeminate; 'real men', often working-class youth; and 'fjollor', flamboyant queens. Three identities, perhaps? But Nilsson also shows how the patterns of homosexual life grew out of the structure of the industrial and maritime city. Among the conditions shaping sexuality were crowded housing, a sharp gender division of labour, high density of men in public spaces, a non-respectable working-class street life, connections to other cities via the shipping trade, certain patterns of policing, and the poverty of many young men, who might enter homosexual relationships for a period and then move on.

The distinctive forms of homosexual practice changed as these conditions changed. The 1950s saw rising affluence in Sweden, suburban working-class housing, the growth of the welfare state, and moral panics about the seduction of youth. A sharper cultural distinction between heterosexual and homosexual people followed the increasing privacy of

sexual conduct itself. Thus the configurations of sexual and social practice which might easily be read as 'identities' were dependent on historically transitory social conditions, and for many participants were only
a limited part of their whole sexual life-history.

A study such as Nilsson's gives a real-life relevance to the theoretical
ideas of deconstructionism. Deconstructionist gender theory, particularly
influential in the United States, has questioned the stability of all identity
categories, paying attention to the ruses of language through which an
impression of solidity and essence are created for such categories as
'woman' or 'gay'. Analyses of gender performativity do not require the
identity concept at all.

Given such problems with the idea of identity, is the concept worth
anything? Certainly the word has been massively over-used. It often
serves merely as a pretentious synonym for self, reputation or social
standing.

In some cases, to use the term 'identity' for a configuration of gender
or sexual practice may be actively misleading. Guy Hocquenghem (1972),
one of the most brilliant theorists of Gay Liberation, argued that homosexual desire is *in principle* inchoate, anarchic, an impersonal flux not a
personal unity. Homosexual desire is desire that escapes being 'oedipalized', that is, organized by the patriarchal social order. Homosexuality
is, in a sense, the opposite of an identity, being desire and practice that
cannot be welded into a unity.

A great deal of *heterosexual* desire also fails to be 'oedipalized'.
Heterosexual desire, too, is often perverse, transitory, unbounded, and
pushes against the social authority that constructs fixed positions and
bounded identities in a heterosexual order. As Lynne Segal puts it in
Straight Sex (1994: 254–5): 'Sexual relations are perhaps the most
fraught and troubling of all social relations precisely because, especially
when heterosexual, they so often *threaten* rather than confirm gender
polarity.' For instance, it is precisely in sex that heterosexual men are
most likely to experience dependence, uncertainty, passivity and – quite
simply – shared experience with women.

To Erikson there was never any doubt that it was desirable to have a
unified identity. He saw that as a task to be accomplished in the course
of growing up. Most other people who have written about identity have
also assumed that everybody ought to have one. But is this really so
desirable? Some identities are pretty revolting – at least in their consequences for others; racist skinheads and tobacco corporation executives
come to mind.

To weld one's personality into a united whole is to refuse internal
diversity and openness. It may also be to refuse change. Major reform
in gender relations may well require a de-structuring of the self, an ex-

perience of gender vertigo, as part of the process. I found this for the group of men in the Australian 'green' movement who were trying to change traditional masculinity. The American sociologist Barbara Risman (1998) has found a comparable experience in 'fair families' (i.e. gender-equal families) in the United States. But how far can this go? I now turn to the extreme cases recognized in gender studies. And this may provoke some re-thinking of the 'identity' problem.

Third gender, transgender, transsexual

One of the most dramatic proofs of the importance of social processes in gender, and a familiar disproof of biological essentialism, is the fact that different societies have recognized different gender categories. There are not only women and men; there might also be third genders, or variations on two that seem to multiply the gender categories in which people can live.

This question has intrigued gender researchers, and there is a large ethnographic literature addressed to categories such as the 'berdache', the 'two-souled' people of indigenous cultures in the south-western region of North America (Williams 1986), who have male bodies, a social position closer to that of women than of men, and great spiritual power. Javanese society traditionally provided a space for 'banci', people with male bodies and women's dress who typically have sex with straight men. In Brazil there are groups who are physically male, and have sex with men within a sexual culture that makes a strong distinction between the insertive and the receptive partner. The one who penetrates maintains his masculinity, while the one who is penetrated is no longer exactly a man, though may also not regard herself/himself as fully a woman (Parker 1991).

These groups are all different from each other, and whether the idea of a 'third gender' makes sense for any of them is debated. Certainly all are vulnerable to change. In North America, the Spanish colonizers regarded them with religious horror and tried to stamp out such indige-nous customs, with considerable brutality. In contemporary Indonesia, 'banci' communities are distinct from a new sexual category, 'gay' men, who have emerged in more affluent social contexts with stronger links to North American gay culture (Oetomo 1996). Brazil has also seen the arrival of a 'gay' model of reciprocal sexuality. In the gay pattern, both partners are both insertive and receptive, and both regard themselves fully as men.

Dennis Altman, in an important survey of contemporary sexuality, *Global Sex* (2001), points out that such changes are not necessarily the simple substitution of a 'Western' sexuality for a 'traditional' sexuality. Globalization involves an enormously complex interaction between sexual customs and gender regimes that are in any case diverse and divided. The result is a spectrum of sexual practices and categories, formed in contexts of cultural disruption and economic inequality.

This is strikingly shown in Thailand. In research by Peter Jackson (1997), the traditional Thai sex/gender categories for males were 'phuchai' (man, mainly heterosexual) and 'kathoey' (effeminate or cross-gender, receptive homosexual). Under the impact of international gay culture, these categories have not disappeared. Rather, they have been elaborated with a series of additions: 'bai' (bisexual), 'gay-king' (homosexual, preferring to be insertor), 'gay-queen' (usually effeminate, preferring to be receptive) and 'gay-quing' (masculine or effeminate, and sexually versatile).

The gender order of the metropole, originating in western Europe, serves in contemporary globalization mainly as a model of gender dichotomy. The two genders are mostly assumed to be heterosexual, though the gender dichotomy is also maintained in the way Western culture deals with male-to-male or female-to-female sex. 'Lesbian' and 'gay' are well-established categories; 'bisexual', by contrast, is an unstable category with no clear social meaning.

But this gender order does have complications. According to the cultural historian Thomas Laqueur (1990), before about the eighteenth century CE, European culture did not have a dichotomous model of male and female bodies as natural opposites; rather, the female tended to be seen as a kind of imperfect male. Even within a dichotomous gender symbolism, there are many opportunities for violating the boundaries, whether in a carnival mood or with great seriousness. A well-known study by Marjorie Garber, *Vested Interests* (1992), finds an astonishing range of cross-dressing practices, in theatre, film, the sex industry, religion, music, detective stories, television . . . ranging from Marlene Dietrich's top hat to Boy George's dresses. So many, in fact, that Garber sees drag as a major expression of contemporary cultural anxiety.

The carnival end of this spectrum can be understood as entertainment and relief – it is no accident that most of Garber's examples come from the worlds of fiction and performance. It is the serious end of the spectrum that poses the difficulties, and perhaps the opportunities, for gender theory. People who somehow *live* across gender boundaries, who don't just dip in and out, have intrigued gender analysts within Western culture as much as 'third gender' categories have intrigued ethnographers.

From the earliest days of scientific research on sexuality and gender, such people have appeared in the pages of research monographs as a kind of interesting monster. Richard von Krafft-Ebing, whose disdainful

Psychopathia Sexualis (1886) was both a founding text of medico-legal sexology and a considerable under-the-counter best-seller, collected lurid cases of 'mental hermaphroditism'. The genial Havelock Ellis devoted over 100 pages of his *Studies in the Psychology of Sex* (1928) to 'Eonism', his name for thorough-going gender inversion (after a French aristocrat, the Chevalier d'Eon, who had at different times presented as a man and as a woman). Even the great Sigmund Freud (1911) did it; his discussion of the case of Dr Schreber examines gender-change beliefs as part of an analysis of psychosis.

After psychoanalysis and the social science of gender were well developed, 'transsexuals', as such people came to be called in the 1950s, still appeared to psychiatrists and sociologists as a kind of natural experiment exposing the mechanisms of the gender system. One American transsexual woman, given the pseudonym Agnes, became the subject of a minor industry, stretching across three academic disciplines.

The story of the creation of 'transsexualism' as a medical syndrome, the ambiguous role of doctors and the controversy within the medical profession is well told in some accessible texts (King 1981, Califia 2003), and interested readers can find many of the key documents in Susan Stryker and Stephen Whittle's admirable *Transgender Studies Reader* (2006). Here I will focus on three issues that seem particularly relevant to understanding the gender order.

The first issue is whether transsexual lives really are the natural experiment many researchers have taken them to be, revealing truths about how gender works. Are West and Zimmerman (1987) right when they say the case of Agnes 'makes visible what culture has made invisible – the accomplishment of gender'?

The answer is yes, in the sense that Agnes did study the gender practices of the women around her, and put them into operation. Of course you don't have to be transsexual to make such a study; anthropologists and teenagers do it all the time. To the extent that one's gender position is a matter of how one is recognized in everyday interaction, transsexual lives do dramatize the process, since that recognition is likely to be problematic, needing to be worked at.

But the answer is no, in the stronger sense that West and Zimmerman mean 'accomplishment'. In their analysis, gender is made performatively in the 'doing' that allows other people to assign one to a gender category. The whole point of Agnes' dilemma was that she was *already* a woman – she thought of herself as a woman, she had the corresponding interests and desires and appearance, she expected to be recognized as such. Being a woman was, in Agnes' life, a fact. But she was a young woman with some serious problems, including having a penis, and that was why she went to the doctors and asked for surgery. She had indeed been 'passing', *as a boy*, in her earlier life, in accordance with the social classification of her body as male. It was intolerable contradiction that had driven her to start making a bodily transition. (Which she did, famously, by finding an illicit source of oestrogen while still going through puberty.)

If transsexual lives uniquely illustrate any truth about the foundations of the gender order, it is perhaps the force of the contradictions that can arise in gender processes.

This leads immediately to the second question, about the 'fluidity' of gender. With the rise of performative theories of gender, there has been great interest in shifts, transitions, variations in gender and violations of norms. If normative gender is brought into being performatively, then, by changing the performative actions, we should be able to create non-normative gender. Hence the many displays of transgender positions, attempts to tangle the masculine and the feminine, or even to explode right out of the gender system. Hence the fascination, in cultural studies, with body modifications of various kinds. Are not transsexual women and men, reversing their original gender assignment, undertaking severe body changes, the most striking possible proof of the fluidity of gender?

Again, the answer is yes in one sense and no in another. Transsexual experience and practice, and the professional and public debates that have swirled around them, are indeed a site of complexity in the gender order. The medical researchers spent a lot of time trying to classify transvestites, pseudo-transsexuals, true transsexuals, homosexuals, effeminate men, masculine women and sub-categories of each; and none of these efforts ever produced a stable classification. A well-informed (though anti-transition) psychiatrist commented that in this field there is not even a spectrum of gender positions, there is a 'magma', a molten mass like the core of a volcano (Chiland 2003).

But in another sense, the transsexual 'cases' that Chiland herself talks about are a dramatic proof of the *lack* of fluidity, the stability, indeed the *intransigence* of gender. One of the most striking features of the autobiographies that transsexual women and men have written, and the life-history interviews they have given, is the repeated declaration that, in a strong sense, they have always been like this. This is abundantly clear in the best social-scientific study of the process of gender transition, Henry Rubin's *Self-Made Men* (2003). The gender project, to use the term introduced earlier in this chapter, is consistent over time – however 'wrong' in terms of conventional social embodiment it may be. Hence the sensation of being trapped in the wrong body, narrated in auto-biographies such as Katherine Cummings' *Katherine's Diary* (1992).

What does change, in the turns and twists in transsexual lives, is how one deals with this intractable problem, this impossible embodiment.

Women and men undertaking gender transitions, if they are very lucky, will find great support, but, if they are not lucky, will face ostracism, loss of jobs, and family hostility, as well as major difficulties in sexual relations. Many younger transsexual women have to support themselves by sex work such as stripping and prostitution. As Harriet (chapter 2) found, there is a certain clientele of straight men who are excited by transsexual women. But this does not mean they respect them. Roberta Perkins' (1983) pioneering book presenting the voices of transsexual women in Sydney includes Naomi, a stripper who remarked:

> I think men have a definite dislike for women in general, that's why women are raped and bashed, and strippers are up there to provide an outlet for this dislike by the yelling of profanities at them. Transsexuals are lower down than women according to men, and look how many men sexually abuse transsexuals. (1983: 73)

This brings me to the third issue: politics. There have been in the past sharp differences over the significance of transsexual experience for gender politics, some commentators seeing gender conservatism and some seeing gender revolution.

In a very strange development, in contemporary human rights talk 'transsexuals' are now treated as a de-gendered identity group. In this discourse, 'transsexuals' (now no longer named as men or women) became a 'T' in an amazing new acronym LGBTTI, listing 'sexual minorities' in need of rights protection (lesbian, gay, bisexual, transgender, transsexual, intersex). Regardless of the logical incoherence of this list, units about this grouping have been added to gender studies programmes in universities, and declarations about them are made in policy statements about discrimination.

In the United States especially, the term 'transgender community' came into use, as if a stable group had been formed which either could follow the familiar model of identity politics, or could be regarded as the epitomy of queer, of gender refusal. It was almost as if an attempt were being made to create a third-gender category in the heart of the global metropole. I hope the people involved in this brave project do find, or make, a liveable space. It may be helpful to keep the term 'transgender' for this project, and the group that forms around it.

But that is rather different from the process of *transition* for which the term 'transsexual' was invented. Viviane Namaste in *Invisible Lives* (2000) challenges transgender discourse, urging attention to the real-life experiences, subjectivities and struggles of transsexual men and women that are 'erased' by queer theory as well as by government agencies. Simply accessing health care and social services, as Namaste's research in Canada shows, can be very difficult for people making transitions.

Coming back to the original question, gender transition does have a deep connection with the revolutionary potential in human life (though no-one would or should undertake transition as a political gesture). Being a transsexual woman and a committed feminist is perfectly consistent. The reader may have noticed that I use the term 'transsexual' only as an adjective, not as a noun (except when quoting other views). The basic idea is a process, not a social group or a type of person. But gender transition only happens through severe contradictions in personal life. These can be unbearable (there is a high rate of suicide among people in this situation), commonly absorb a great deal of energy simply to hold together, and can be made much harder, as Namaste says, by denial of recognition from institutions or movements. Somewhere there are links between the potential and the reality, but we don't yet have them.

7

Gender on the large scale

Most discussions of gender concern the personal: issues such as identities, motherhood and child-rearing, family life, sexuality, and their pathologies, such as prejudice, domestic violence and rape. We have already seen reasons to go beyond this. To understand personal relations, we must take into account institutions, economies, ideologies and governments. Chapter 5 outlined an approach to the structure of gender relations. This chapter applies the same approach to gender relations on the very large scale: in corporations, governments and global society.

The gendered corporation

The corporation is the dominant form of economic organization in contemporary society, the key institution of developed capitalism. There were 5.7 million corporations in the United States in 2005, according to taxation statistics. Most were small, but more than 2,000 held assets over $2.5 billion dollars each. Transnational corporations are the main players in the international economy. The biggest have workforces in the hundreds of thousands, such as Toyota with 299,000 workers in 2007; profits (and sometimes losses) in the tens of billions, such as Exxon Mobil with $39.5 billion profit in 2007; and annual revenues bigger than the entire national product of small countries.

Corporations are gendered institutions, with a gendered history. 'Companies' of merchants in early modern Europe were entirely composed of men. When ownership began to be divided up and became itself a kind of commodity, with the creation of joint-stock companies and the first stock exchanges in the seventeenth and eighteenth centuries, these too were socially defined as men's institutions. The creation of the modern form of capital was thus part of the historical process that created a masculinized public realm, which also included the emerging liberal state, and organs of public opinion such as the press.

This went for a long time unquestioned. When, in the nineteenth century, middle-class women in the rich countries challenged their exclusion from universities and the professions, there was no comparable demand for entry to business management. The gender pattern of the corporation itself only came into focus in the 1970s, when liberal and academic feminism challenged organization theory. The change is marked by the work of Rosabeth Kanter in the United States, whose *Men and Women of the Corporation* appeared in 1977. Kanter criticized the absence of gender awareness in organization research, and showed how gender issues mattered, even for the minority of women who did make it into the corporate hierarchy.

Over the next three decades, social research on corporate life accumulated, and a theory of 'gendered organizations' emerged in the global metropole. Some of the studies have already been mentioned: Hochschild's (1983) research on 'emotion work' in airlines and debt agencies, and Pringle's (1989) study of secretaries. Some of the best research has focused on the world of manual workers in large-scale industries. The sociologist Miriam Glucksmann wrote a wonderful account of British factory life in *Women on the Line* (1982). This was based on seven months' participant observation in a motor vehicle component assembly plant, and gives a vivid picture of the corporate hierarchy, daily life on the shop floor, and the connections with home life. There was a rigid gender division of labour in this plant. Women were employed in the low-paid routine jobs only, promotion was blocked, men could get twice the wage for doing easier jobs: 'It was obvious that the only qualification you needed for a better job was to be a man.' The women were disillusioned about men, and supported each other in daily conflicts with male supervisors. But their poverty, fatigue, household demands and the gender segregation of working-class life made effective organizing almost impossible.

Gender divisions are equally strong in corporate agriculture, which is now transforming rural life across the world. A fascinating oral-history study in Chile by Heidi Tinsman (2000) describes the export-oriented fruit industry created under the Pinochet dictatorship. The companies engaged in this business recruited women workers on a large scale. But the consequences were not all as expected. Rural women's command of an income and ability to make shopping trips and purchasing decisions changed the balance of power with husbands. The segregated work groups created by the employers provided an alternative to domestic isolation, and led to new relationships among women. In both respects, the process eroded the dictatorship's official maternalist ideology.

Gender hierarchies are not just 'tradition'; they are in many cases deliberately introduced and actively defended. That was shown in Cynthia Cockburn's classic study of British printing workers, *Brothers* (1983). David Collinson, David Knights and Margaret Collinson in *Managing to Discriminate* (1990) found the same thing in British white-collar work in the insurance industry. For instance, a manager opposed to promoting women justified his hostility by the idea (possibly correct!) that the customers, also men, would not like it.

Research such as this underpinned the development of a theory of gendered organizations, which emerged at the end of the 1980s in the work of Joan Acker in the United States, Peta Tancred in Canada, Clare Burton in Australia, and British researchers such as the Collinsons and Jeff Hearn (collected in Mills and Tancred's *Gendering Organizational Analysis*, 1992). The key idea was that gender discrimination is not an accidental feature of a basically gender-neutral bureaucracy, that can be fixed by changing a few attitudes. Gender is a structural feature of corporate life, linked to gender relations in other sectors of society, that shapes job definitions, understandings of 'merit' and promotion, management techniques, marketing and a whole lot more.

The analysis of gender in workplaces has become steadily more sophisticated since those beginnings, with increasing attention to the extent of unintentional gendering, and the dynamic character of gender at the level of personal interaction within organizations (Martin 2006). A classic example is provided by a study of Italian corporations by Sylvia Gherardi and Barbara Poggio (2001). Women were arriving at a management level here; but as they did, a 'dance' of adjustment and compromise occurred, and the gender order seemed to close around them.

In the United States, significant numbers of women have now reached middle management, and there is endless discussion of the 'glass ceiling' which prevents their getting into top-level management. In 1991 the US Congress set up a 21-person Glass Ceiling Commission to investigate the problem. They found that, among the biggest corporations in the United States, 97 per cent of senior managers were White, and 95 to 97 per cent were men. Of the top 1,000 companies, 2 had women CEOs. That is, one-fifth of 1 per cent of big corporations had a woman in the top job. This was cited as a sign of progress.

The Commission attributed this situation to a set of 'barriers' which prevent access to high places. They include: unsuitable or inadequate educational background; prejudice and bias on the part of men in power;

career paths that divert women from the main promotion pipeline; poor anti-discrimination enforcement by government; inadequate information about the problem; inadequate publicity; and fear of loss among White men in middle management. Evidently the reasons for the absence of women and minority men from top management have to do with broad features of business organizations, and deeply entrenched patterns of division in the workplace – just as the sociologists had been saying. Commenting on the prevailing culture of US business, the Commission (1995: 34) quoted the CEO of a retail firm:

> The old-line companies are run by the white '46 long' guys who practice inappropriate male rituals that are dysfunctional to business. Male bonding through hunting, fishing and sports talk is irrelevant to business. Too much so-called 'strategic planning' takes place after the bars close – that kind of male fellowship ritual is irrelevant to business.

As the remedy for all this, the Glass Ceiling Commission proposed – a change of attitude! They tried to persuade capitalists to see that a more diverse management team would be *Good for Business* (the title of their main report). That is, they relied on the profit motive to drive a massive voluntary reconstruction of business management – somehow failing to notice that the profit motive has been operating full blast since the dawn of capitalism, so far resulting in a management group 97 per cent White and 95 per cent to 97 per cent men. The US government subsequently lost interest in the problem.

There is no reason to think the picture in other industrialized countries is very different. But the response sometimes is. Norway has now passed a law requiring corporations to have women making at least 40 per cent of their boards of directors, and setting other targets for gender change in the corporate sector. The effects have yet to be seen.

Managerial masculinities do change over time. The British historian Michael Roper (1994), in a fascinating book called *Masculinity and the British Organization Man since 1945*, traces changes in the management of British manufacturing firms. An older generation of managers had a hands-on relation with the production process, identified themselves closely with the firm and the quality of the product, and took a paternalistic interest in the engineering workers. With the growing power of finance capital in the British economy, a new cadre of managers has appeared. They are also men, but are more oriented to accountancy and profit, less interested in technology and the product, and not very much interested in the workers. A more generic, and more ruthless, managerial masculinity has taken over.

Capitalism is a turbulent economic system; markets expand and collapse, industries rise and fall, corporations restructure themselves in search of profit. One of the most important of these changes, the rise of transnational corporations, will be considered later in the chapter; here I will simply note that transnational management grew out of management structures in the rich countries of the global metropole. The kind of change mapped by Roper seems to be common. The notorious case of the Enron Corporation, the Texas-based pipeline company that became a huge 'new economy' energy trader, and collapsed with a huge stink in 2001, is an example. Enron epitomized the style of hard-driving, profit-centred management that had little respect for its workforce or for business ethics, provided it could rake in profits and bonuses (Fox 2003). A similar kind of masculinity appears in studies of financial trading floors, though as Peter Levin (2001) notes, it is expressed in different ways depending on fluctuations in the pace of work.

When Rosabeth Kanter studied women in corporations in the 1970s, she found that the social pressures they were under tended to reinforce traditional femininity. When Judy Wajcman (1999) studied both women and men managers in globally oriented high-technology firms in the 1990s, she found the women were under heavy pressure to act just like the men: work the long hours, fight in the office wars, put pressure on their subordinates and focus on profit. In order to survive in this world, the women managers had to restructure their domestic lives so they too could shed responsibilities for child care, cooking and housework. Wajcman found no truth in the widespread belief that women coming into management would bring a more caring, nurturant or humane style to the job. It is not surprising that she called her book *Managing Like a Man*.

From the point of view of gender justice, the picture in top management looks bleak. The picture is equally bleak when we look at the owners of big capital. Mike Donaldson and Scott Poynting, in *Ruling Class Men* (2007), pulled together many sources of information to draw a picture of the social life and culture of the corporate rich, and the picture is not pretty. These men have lives that are materially privileged but socially cut off, have family relationships where women are mostly consigned to being decorative and producing heirs, and practice a deliberate 'toughening' of the young men who will take control of family fortunes.

What about the situation lower down the hierarchy, among the people who actually do the corporations' labour? Here the situation is unquestionably more varied, as corporations have assembled socially diverse workforces. An excellent world-wide review of ethnographies of workplace gender, put together by Winifred Poster (2002), emphasizes not only the use of gender division and gender stereotyping as means of control, but the great variety of situations in which gender is constructed. Racial hierarchies, sexualization, class distinctions, are all operating in the making of workplace masculinities and femininities – as would be expected from the 'intersection' theory discussed in chapter 5.

What of the institutions that represent workers' interests in battles with corporate power – the unions? Here too we find patriarchal organizations. The union movement originated mainly in men's occupations. Though there have been some famous episodes in union organizing among women, such as the London 'matchgirls' strike' in 1888, union membership has remained predominantly men, and union leadership overwhelmingly men. The difficulty of establishing a voice for women in the union movement, even in a country like Australia where both unionism and feminism have been strong, is documented in Suzanne Franzway's *Sexual Politics and Greedy Institutions* (2000). Resistance from union men, embodying an old, combative style of working-class masculinity, has been a constant problem. Yet as the economy has changed, women have been a rising proportion of the union membership. The latest two presidents of the Australian Council of Trade Unions (the unions' peak organization) have been women.

The gendered state

Most of the world's presidents, prime ministers, cabinet ministers, generals and civil service managers are men. Women gained legal status, and the right to vote, much later than men – and in some parts of the world still do not have legal equality. There are obvious reasons, then, why the state would be seen as a patriarchal institution. In the 1970s and 1980s, feminists in the metropole made a number of attempts to formulate a theory of the patriarchal state. Its main themes can be summed up in six points.

- The state is the core of the wider structure of power relations in gender. Traditional theories of the state in philosophy and political science said nothing about gender because they could not see gender where only men were present, where no 'difference' was visible. But where only men are present, we are looking at a powerful gender effect – that is, the total exclusion of women!
- The state has a well-marked internal gender regime. There is an overall gender division of labour, with men concentrated in departments such as the military, police, infrastructure and economic agencies, women concentrated in social welfare, health and education.

The centres of state power, the top decision-making units, are heavily masculine, and women's interests are represented in more peripheral agencies than men's interests.

- The state makes policies concerned with gender issues. As these policies are put into effect, the state regulates gender relations in the wider society. This is not a minor aspect of what the state does. It involves many policy areas, from housing through education to criminal justice and the military.

- This activity not only regulates existing gender relations. The state's activity also helps to *constitute* gender relations and form gender identities. An important example is the role of repressive laws and state-backed medicine in creating the category of 'the homosexual' in the late nineteenth century. The categories of 'husband' and 'wife' are also partly constituted by state action, through mechanisms ranging from marriage laws to tax policy.

- Because of these activities and capacities, the state is the key target in gender politics. It is the focus of most political mobilization on gender issues, as pressure groups and popular movements try to reach their goals via the state. Indeed, the rise of the liberal state was the focus of a historic change in the form of gender politics, which became mass politics for the first time in the nineteenth century.

- Since gender relations are marked by crisis tendencies and structural change, the state as the heart of gendered power is itself liable to crisis and change. Crisis tendencies which impinge on the state include problems of legitimation to do with men's violence, and tensions arising from the gender division of labour ('equal opportunity' and the 'glass ceiling' for women).

These conclusions were drawn from a considerable amount of research on politics and bureaucracies, and they have a certain solidity and realism. But they also have limitations, which are easier to see now, especially when we look beyond the global metropole.

First, the state is only one of society's centres of power. A traditional definition of the state is the institution that holds a monopoly of the legitimate use of force in a given territory. But this ignores the domestic violence of husbands towards wives, a widespread practice which used to be wholly legitimate and which only recently has been broadly contested.

Can we regard husbands as a 'power'? Conventional political analysis does not recognize a husbands' party. In a patriarchal gender order, however, husbands' interests in their wives' sexual and domestic services are institutionalized on a society-wide basis. This is a power to which state agencies have repeatedly accommodated. Wendy Hollway (1994) documents this fact in a study of Tanzanian civil service employment. Tanzania had an official policy of equal conditions for men and women in public employment, as most countries now do. But this policy was subverted when it clashed with husbands' interests. For instance, women civil servants were sent on training programmes only if their husbands had given approval: 'Applications without a husband's permission were treated as if [official] permission had been withheld.'

Another kind of power has emerged in the form of security companies. There are said to be more private security agents in the United States now than there are publicly employed police. A substantial part of the armed force used in the US occupation of Iraq has consisted of 'security contractors', between 20,000 and 30,000 mercenary soldiers employed by corporations such as Blackwater Worldwide. Increasing numbers of the affluent, even in rich countries, live in gated communities, that is, housing complexes with fences patrolled by security employees, designed to keep out the poor, the Black and the card-less.

These private security systems are gendered: controlled by men, mostly employing men and, in the case of the gated communities, en-gating women. Because their legitimacy depends on property, not citizenship, private security systems so far have escaped the political pressure for equal opportunity which women have been able to exert on the state. The gendered state, then, operates in a more complex field of forces than might immediately appear.

In discussions of politics, 'gender' is often a code-word for women. But it is essential to bring men and masculinity explicitly into the analysis of the state. Especially in an organization as large and complex as the state, it is important to recognize the distinction between hegemonic and subordinated masculinities (Messerschmidt 1993). The masculinization of the state, accurately identified in feminist theory, is principally a relation-ship between state institutions and hegemonic masculinity.

This principle gives us some help in understanding the masculinization of post-colonial states. In some parts of the world, such as central and western Africa, the state structure left by de-colonization, lacking legiti-macy and often cutting irrationally across geographical and cultural landscapes, has been racked with conflict that has often turned into military coups or internal war. The heavily masculinized military forces of the colonial era thus provided the core of the post-colonial state elites – notably so in the richest country in the region, Nigeria. In cases like Algeria, Zimbabwe and Cuba, the leadership of guerrilla forces gained control of the post-colonial state and set up authoritarian regimes. Even where a civilian leadership remained in control, as in India, the attempt to hold together a new republic and the drive for economic development valorized a hegemonic masculinity that was focused on authority and rational calculation, suppressed emotions, and was capable of rolling over local communities and traditions. (At least, that is how I interpret Ashis Nandy's critique of the modernizing state [Nandy 1987].)

The Turkish state, the first modern republic in the Islamic world, was a particularly important model. General Mustafa Kemal, a hero of the First World War, came to power at a time of absolute crisis, drove out occupying forces in what amounted to a war of independence, and led a modernizing elite in setting up a secular state. Emancipation of women was on his agenda, and women now have a presence in the Turkish state greater than in Arab countries; yet a masculinized military has remained a dominant force in the republic. As Sinclair-Webb (2000) shows in a very interesting ethnographic study, military service in Turkey is a rite of passage into manhood, connected with national identity. But it is also a site of tension: professional soldiers, especially the officers, regard the conscripts as poor material. The army, that is to say, does not rely on an already-established masculinity, but tries to shape young men in a new mould. This agenda is, however, running into difficulty – partly from the Kurdish rebellion, partly from the rise of political Islam, and partly from cultural change among youth.

The state is not only a mechanism of authority and force. It is also the site where social interests are articulated and rights claimed. 'Manhood suffrage' was the goal of democratic movements in nineteenth-century Europe, connected with the idea of a family wage and the working man as head-of-household. State guarantees of civil rights provided the context for the emergence of alternative masculinities in the metropole in the later twentieth century. Homosexual masculinities provide the best known example. Equally interesting is the institution of *Zivildienst*, civilian service, introduced in 1973 as an alternative to military conscription in Germany, which recognized committed non-violent masculinities. It is now chosen by more young men than military service.

Equally we need to acknowledge the complexity of women's relationships with the state. Julia O'Connor, Ann Orloff and Sheila Shaver in *States, Markets, Families* (1999) survey gender and welfare policy in four industrialized countries. They confirm how apparently gender-neutral policies actually have gender effects. For instance, retirement income systems may make better provision for people who have a continuous employment career (who happen to be mostly men) than for people who have done a lot of unpaid domestic work (mostly women). It is clear that the women's movement has been a force in welfare debates but its influence has been uneven. Different areas of state policy may show different gender patterns. The United States, for instance, has relatively poor income security for women, but relatively strong legal support for women's 'body rights'.

Much of state policy in relation to gender concerns controls over women's bodies, and these can be difficult to change. Mala Htun (2003), in a study of gender politics in Argentina, Brazil and Chile, shows that, while women's rights fluctuated under the dictatorships and with the transition to democracy, in no case were abortion rights improved. It therefore becomes very interesting to consider the theory of the 'woman-friendly state' advanced by some feminist theorists in Scandinavia. Borchorst and Siim (2002), reviewing this theory, note the break from feminist pessimism about the state. A combination of feminist mobilization from below, and laws mandating gender equity from above, produces a regime much more favourable to women's interests. Politics does matter.

A feminist presence within the state is found in other parts of the world too. In Australia, where this is a major form of gender politics, the officials responsible for gender equality are known charmingly as 'femocrats'. Their story is vividly told in *Inside Agitators* (1996) by Hester Eisenstein, who spent some time as a femocrat herself, and they have certainly had influence in education, employment rights and some other policy fields. But their influence waned with the rise of the new right and neoliberalism.

Similarly, a comparative study by Philomina Okeke-Ihejirika and Susan Franceschet (2002) points to specific conditions for the success of 'state feminism'. In Chile, women were prominent in the struggle against the Pinochet dictatorship. In the transition to democracy, feminists had access to the top levels of state power. But in Nigeria, though women were involved in the struggle for independence and feminist groups have persisted, the post-independence regimes had no place for feminist ideas. Instead, they promoted tame women's organizations led by the wives of the real rulers – borrowing the US idea of the 'first lady' – which pursued a mild welfare agenda and a conservative view of women's place.

As in Nigeria, it is common that anti-colonial, nationalist or revolutionary movements mobilize women's support. The Chinese revolution is perhaps the best-known case. The Maoist slogan 'women hold up half the sky' was part of an attack on feudal attitudes and laws which had enforced the subordination of women (Stacey 1983). But establishing a post-colonial or post-revolutionary regime has often meant installing a new version of patriarchy. Women have been brought into the labour force, but not equally into the political leadership. Maria Mies (1986) sardonically observes how post-colonial regimes symbolized the new patriarchy with cults of revolutionary Founding Fathers – including Mao. When the government of the new republic of Nepal came into existence in 2008, it was eerie to see posters showing the genealogy of the ruling party – a row of male faces from Marx via Stalin to Mao. Not a woman among them.

In some cases the exclusion of women is explicit. Yemen (since its reunification) has been described as the most oppressive country in the world for women, though Saudi Arabia runs it close. The Wahhabi sect of Islam that predominates in this region is as implacably opposed to women having authority as the Catholic sect of Christianity is to women being priests. Nayereh Tohidi's (1991) narrative of feminist politics in Shi'ite Iran shows how assertive attitudes among women there were seen as evidence of the corruption of religion and culture by Western influences. In other cases the exclusion of women is a matter of practice, not dogma. Most post-colonial states have been dependent on multinational corporations, so have been operating in an economic environment dominated by men. Singapore, one of the striking success stories of dependent capitalist development, has also created one of the most monolithic patriarchies in post-colonial government.

Yet the current is not all one way. There is also a history of women's activism in Muslim countries. In certain cases – Pakistan, Turkey and Indonesia – women have become prominent political leaders. The post-colonial state in India has provided a political environment in which a strong feminist movement could develop. And it is striking that, of the five successor states to the British Indian empire, three have had women prime ministers and a fourth nearly did. One of these was the first elected woman head of government in the world: Sirimavo Bandaranaike, elected prime minister of Sri Lanka in 1960. The one who was nearly head of government, Aung San Suu Kyi, is (at the time of writing) still in detention because the military men controlling Burma fear her so much.

In the countries which were once the imperial centres and are now the financial centres of the global economy, feminist movements have had a good many legal and constitutional victories. There have been defeats, too, such as the attempt in the 1970s to embed gender equality in the US constitution. Broadly, however, equal formal rights between women and men have been won. They include the right to vote, the right to own property, the right to take legal action, equal employment opportunity, and so on. The old form of state patriarchy, with masculine authority embedded in bureaucratic hierarchies, proved vulnerable to feminist challenge.

But the state has been changing recently, in ways that seem to make power less accountable to women (Yeatman 1990). New agendas of 'reform' have privatized many state services, and make remaining public services operate more like corporations. As Néstor García Canclini (1999: 13) observed, under neoliberalism the main decisions that shape everyday life 'are taken in places that are inaccessible and difficult to identify'.

Women's increased presence in the public realm is now counterbalanced by a decline of the public realm itself, or, as Rachel Simon-Kumar (2004) puts it, a tendency for the state and the market to blur into each other. The key neoliberal policies – deregulating markets, reducing taxes and government services, transferring resources to private business – amount to a relocation of power into institutions dominated by men. The state, in both metropole and periphery, is increasingly integrated into the world of global capitalism. So let us turn to consider how gender works at the largest scale of all, the scale of world society.

Gender in world society

In this section I will discuss what Sarah Radcliffe, Nina Laurie and Robert Andolina (2004) have aptly called 'the transnationalization of gender'. This has become a major theme of debate recently, though there has long been a concern with global issues in feminism. Kartini in Java, at the beginning of the twentieth century, could rely on support from women in the Netherlands, the colonial power (chapter 3). International women's organizations have existed for most of the twentieth century, such as the Women's International League for Peace and Freedom, founded during the First World War and still going today. What we now call 'gender' issues have been debated in international forums since before that war (Lenz, Szypulski and Molsich 1996: 10–12).

Contemporary debates have, however, been re-shaped by the creation of inter-governmental forums specifically for discussing gender inequalities and the interests of women. The United Nations Decade for Women 1975–85 made a remarkable change. In the Decade for Women, and after, a series of high-profile conferences created a global forum for these concerns and crystallized a policy agenda around women's interests. I believe that this reflects an important reality in gender relations today. There are significant features of the gender order which cannot be understood locally, which *require* analysis on a global scale.

It has become commonplace to talk about 'globalization', i.e. about social organization at a planetary level, though the question is still poorly understood (Connell 2007). It is not a long stretch, therefore, to think about gender as a structure of world society. We need not assume that gender is everywhere the same, as early theories of patriarchy did. Indeed it seems much more likely, at present, that the links are loose and the correspondences uneven. That is the picture shown by Poster's (2002) review of workplace gender across the world, mentioned earlier in this chapter. All we need to assume is that significant linkages do exist, and are being created.

Transnationalization is happening in all the structures of gender relations defined in chapter 5. The economic relations between women and men can hardly avoid it, in a time where large percentages of national economies are owned by foreigners, large sections of industry are dependent on foreign trade, and major investment decisions are made by transnational corporations. The politics of gender must be affected, in a time when global competitiveness is pursued via state restructuring and privatization of public services, and when masculinized military, paramilitary and police institutions are coordinated internationally. Emotional relations and sexuality are impacted by migration, population policies and international travel; the international dimension of gender in the HIV/AIDS pandemic is impossible to miss (Mane and Aggleton 2001). The symbolism of gender must be affected, as images of masculinity and femininity circulate on a vast scale in global media (fashion, 'celebrities', professional sports), while gender ideologies from different cultures are interwoven by migration and intermarriage. The links that constitute a global gender order seem to be of two basic types: interaction between local gender orders, and the creation of new arenas of gender relations.

Interaction between gender orders

Imperial conquest, neo-colonialism and the current world systems of power, investment, trade and communication have brought very diverse societies in contact with each other. The gender orders of those societies have consequently also been brought in contact with each other.

As I have emphasized through this book, this has often been a violent and disruptive process. Imperialism included an assault on local gender arrangements which did not fit the colonizers' templates. Missionaries, for instance, tried to stamp out the third-gender 'berdache' tradition in North America, and what they saw as women's promiscuity in Polynesia. The 'muu-muu' dresses sold to thousands of tourists in Hawai'i are far from being indigenous tradition; they are the legacy of male religious authorities' attempts to cover up women's bodies. Local gender arrangements have also been profoundly re-shaped by profit-making enterprises: slavery, indentured labour, land seizure and resettlement. In the contemporary world, the institutions of masculine violence in different parts of the world are linked by an international arms trade that amounted to $US 45.6 billion in 2006 (Stockholm International Peace Research Institute 2008).

The gender practices re-shaped by such means form new patterns which are, so to speak, the first level of a global gender order. They are specific or local, but carry the impress of the broader forces that make a global society. Let me give two examples.

The first is Nadia Kim's (2006) study of Korean immigrant women in the United States. Korea has a long Confucian tradition with an established model of patriarchal, family-based gender relations. This has been under pressure, with South Korea's rapid industrial development and with the impact of global mass media, especially American images of gender relations. Migration to another country further erodes the Confucian model. The women to whom Kim spoke want to have an active economic life for themselves, more gender equality, and men in their lives who show friendliness, rather than authority, and share in the housework. American men seem to them to represent a modern masculinity better than Korean men. Yet there are complications. Younger women especially are likely to criticize the US military presence in Korea, and the behaviour of US soldiers there; and to criticize American men's promiscuity.

An essay by Mai Ghoussoub (2000) on masculinity in Arab media, especially in Egypt, reveals a tenser situation. She starts with two strange episodes: rumours about an Israeli-invented chewing gum that makes Arab men impotent, and the sudden popularity of mediaeval courtship manuals that celebrate sex in the name of Islam. (One of these is well-known in English translation as *The Perfumed Garden*.) Ghoussoub interprets these episodes as signs of a deep cultural disturbance in the post-colonial Middle East about masculinity. The context is slow economic modernization, political turbulence and the military weakness of Arab states in the face of Israel and the United States. The increasing economic and social status of women in Arabic-speaking societies has posed dilemmas for men whose identities are still founded in traditional gender ideologies. The old sex manuals emphasize women's active sexuality; and mass culture also portrays powerful women, such as the heroine of a popular film, *Mission to Tel Aviv*, who turns the tables on the Israelis. There are many signs, as Ghoussoub argues, of 'a chaotic quest for a definition of modern masculinity'.

The interaction of gender orders is not all one-way. I have previously mentioned Ashis Nandy's observation that the creation of the British empire changed masculinities among the British, as well as among the Indians. There is a small but interesting historical literature on the 'imperial pioneer and hunter' as a masculine model (MacKenzie 1987). Yet there is no question that the pressure of the metropole on the gender orders of the global periphery is much stronger than pressure the other way. We should not think of that as a simple 'modernization' of gender. The two examples just discussed, and the wider historical literature on gender and imperialism (Midgley 1998), show turbulence in the process, and sometimes acute tension.

New arenas of gender relations

Imperialism and globalization have created institutions that operate on a world scale. These institutions all have internal gender regimes, and each gender regime has its gender dynamic – interests, gender politics, processes of change. World-spanning institutions thus create new arenas for gender formation and gender dynamics. The most important of these institutions seem to be transnational corporations, the international state, global media and global markets. I will comment on each in turn.

Transnational corporations. Corporations operating in global markets are now the largest business organizations on the planet. They typically have a marked, though complex, gender division of labour in their workforce, as we have seen, and a strongly masculinized management culture.

Possible changes to managerial masculinity in the new context of transnational business have been the topic of recent debate and research. Charlotte Hooper (2000), in a study of the imagery in a business newspaper, found some evidence of a shift away from a tough, hierarchical model towards an emphasis on teamwork and high technology. A small group of interviews with Australian businessmen (Connell and Wood 2005) certainly supported the emphasis on technology, but in other respects found ambiguous evidence of new patterns. The research continues.

What is at stake is shown by a study of an international merger of finance companies in Scandinavia, where gender orders are among the most egalitarian on earth. Janne Tienari and colleagues (2005) conducted interviews with the top executives of the merged firms, and found a remarkable situation. The senior managers were overwhelmingly men, and basically did not want to hear about gender equality problems. They took management to be naturally men's business, 'constructed according to the core family and male-breadwinner model'. The researchers think that the conditions of transnational business intensify the discursive construction of managerial masculinity as competitive, mobile and work-driven – overriding the Scandinavian social discourse of gender equality. If they are right, the outlook for gender relations in the wider world of transnational corporations is not good.

The international state. A striking feature of twentieth-century political history was the growth of agencies that link territorial states without themselves having a territorial base. They include the International Labour Organization, the League of Nations, the United Nations and its various agencies such as the World Bank and the International Monetary Fund, and the Organization for Economic Co-operation and Development. The European Union, equally important, is a more traditional political form: a regional customs union which has partly evolved into a federal state. Regional bodies such as the African Union, the Association of South-East Asian Nations, and Mercosur remain much looser.

All these agencies are gendered, and have gender effects. Mostly their gender regimes copy those of the conventional states that gave rise to them. Being an outgrowth of diplomacy, they are mainly staffed and run by men, as Cynthia Enloe's (1990) study of the diplomatic world showed. Yet women have been moving into the world of international diplomacy; since Enloe's book was written, the United States has had two women as Secretary of State, Madeleine Albright and Condoleezza Rice. Dorota Gierycz (1999) observes, while documenting all-too-familiar gender inequalities in UN agencies, that they often have staffing rules that guarantee geographical diversity, and so have an element of gender multiculturalism. Inter-governmental forums emphasize a formal equality between participants.

I have been at one meeting of the UN Commission on the Status of Women (effectively, a standing committee of the General Assembly) and watched a remarkable ritual. Diplomat after diplomat, most of them men in business suits, stood up in turn and gravely declared their governments' absolute commitment to equality between women and men.

Further, the United Nations organizations adopted the 'femocrat' strategy pioneered in Scandinavia and Australia, and set up internal agencies to pursue this agenda. The leading one is the Division for the Advancement of Women in the UN Secretariat (i.e. the Secretary-General's department). Development aid agencies now generally have women's programmes, and many associated non-government organizations do the same. There is, now, an international policy machinery concerned with gender equality, and at least one very widely known policy document, the UN Convention on the Elimination of All Forms of Discrimination against Women.

Global media. Multinational media corporations circulate film, video, music and news on a very large scale. There are also more decentralized media (post, telegraph, telephone, fax, the Internet, the Web) and their supporting industries. All contain gender arrangements and circulate gender meanings. The newer media and applications, such as Web-based marketing, have a rapidly growing global reach.

Some commentators have seen this as a new frontier for gender change. The Web especially seems to offer infinite opportunities for playing with gender meanings, for re-inventing oneself, adopting new identities, and so on. Certainly websites such as the 'pro-ana' sites for anorexic girls provide an alternative to everyday relationships, and a cultural context for alternative embodiments.

How far this involves progressive change in gender relations, however, is debatable. The Internet is flooded with pornographic spam that promotes extremely reactionary views of gender – women presented as objects of male desire and consumption, men who think their manhood depends on increasing the size of their penis. The celebrity culture that is a staple of the international mass media for women is cartoon-like in its heteronormativity. Sports programming presents an unremitting diet of competitive, muscular masculinity. The modest excursions into change represented by programmes such as *Queer Eye for the Straight Guy* seem marginal in comparison.

Nor have electronic media proved a major arena for cultural integration. The English language is massively dominant on the Internet, and most of the cultural assumptions are North American. The US market shapes international news. Again, there are counter-forces. There is a large Indian film industry that is gaining international audiences; there are television stations such as al-Jazeera; the Chinese government (among others) attempts to control the Internet.

Global markets. It is important to distinguish markets themselves from the individual corporations that operate in them. International markets – capital, commodity, service and labour markets – have an increasing 'reach' into local economies. They are strongly gender-structured and are now (with the political triumph of neoliberalism) very weakly regulated. The gendered character of markets as social institutions is emerging in recent research, that has revealed an aggressive, misogynist culture in areas such as commodities, energy, stock and futures trading.

I will give as one example a passage from an interview with an Australian finance company executive, one of the few women who actually worked as a trader in this environment, at the time when the Australian economy was being 'opened' to international capital movements. Joyce has clear memories of 'that very macho culture of the dealing room', with its long lunches and high alcohol consumption, a milieu where aggressive behaviour 'is just par for the course, that is just acceptable behaviour, and it is not only accepted, it is expected':

In the dealing rooms, oh, full of the macho bravado, and the liar's-poker type environments. Where, you know, they're [saying] how big their positions are – the bragging, the womanizing, the whole bit. And all of which is entirely forgiven because they make a load of money ... it attracts a certain type of person. [How did Joyce survive in this environment?] I ran a futures book. Futures isn't sexy these days, but they were [then] at the sexy end of the market, they were sophisticated, and people didn't really understand what you were doing ... So they could have thought I was a green tree frog, I knew I was making money. So to that extent the simplicity of the performance criteria goes your way. But the culture was very very hostile ... You'd get the whole kit-and-caboodle, you know: the nude posters went up, and all this sort of stuff, the comment on everything you wore, and everything you did.

Her picture is like that emerging from some US research on traders (Levin 2001). There is still a lot to be done before this is confirmed as an international picture; but on the early indications, the spread of market relationships under neoliberalism is not looking like a paradigm of gender equality.

In these four arenas we can detect elements of an emerging world gender order. It is imperfectly linked up, and far from homogeneous, but is already an important presence. Its weight in our lives will undoubtedly grow.

In chapter 1, I presented some of the statistics of gender inequality and toxicity on a world scale. The measures are fairly rough, and hardly ever go beyond the crude classification of people into 'men' and 'women'. But they are what we currently know. If we had to describe, on a postcard to a being from another galaxy, the state of gender justice among humans in the early twenty-first century CE, what would we say?

The great majority of the very rich and powerful on planet Earth are men. They compete among each other for more wealth and power, and mobilize workforces of both men and women to do so. There is a good deal of violence on the planet, most of it by men, and a good part of it from armed forces, police and prison systems, overwhelmingly composed of men. Women's average incomes are a little over half of men's average incomes, less than that in the poorest countries. As well as doing an increasing amount of wage labour, women do most of the world's caregiving and unpaid domestic labour, and most of the work of bringing up young children. Masculinities and femininities are generally constructed around these conditions, and many of the planet's inhabitants accept them without protest. People who violate accepted patterns of masculinity and femininity often suffer, and are sometimes killed. In many parts of the world men hold power within the household, and there are few places where women do; but negotiation often equalizes domestic relationships in practice. Most of the authority figures in religion, science and the arts are men; women are allocated specific and usually limited roles in those spheres. However, women's access to education has been rising world-wide for the last two generations. This has gone so far that, in rich countries, young women's levels of education now exceed men's. In these countries women's health and expectation of life is also, on average, better than men's. The balance of power and benefit is far from equal, world-wide, but it is more equal than it was in earlier generations.

Hmm, a long postcard. But perhaps this gives a basis for thinking about the political processes that have brought us to this point, and may take us beyond it.

8

Gender politics

Personal politics

In 1997 Pam Benton, whose partner I had been for twenty-nine years, died of breast cancer. Breast cancer is almost entirely a women's disease. The medical specialists who treat it, however, are mostly men – as medical specialists mostly are in Australia. And they, naturally enough, have many of the attitudes and styles of interaction that men in the professions are likely to have.

Early in the treatment, Pam was referred to a prominent Sydney oncologist. Oncology is specialization in cancer, especially in its treatment through chemotherapy, the use of toxic drugs. This gentleman delivered himself of the opinion that if women would use their breasts for what they were intended for, they would not have so much trouble. Pam was furious, and did not consult him again.

There is, as the oncologist well knew, research evidence that rates of breast cancer are lower in women who have had babies early in life and have breast-fed. That is, so to speak, impersonal fact. (Though even with impersonal fact one may ask why researchers should have been concerned with that particular question rather than studying, say, cancer-causing chemicals in the environment.) The research finding was made into a gender insult – which the oncologist probably did not even realize was offensive – by his bland presumption that what women are 'for' is bearing babies. To him, if they had a different pattern of life, they were asking for what they got.

I tell this story not to attack doctors – I could tell of another senior medical man involved in Pam's treatment who was a model of thoughtfulness and care – but to emphasize how intimate and unavoidable gender politics is.

Some issues about power and inequality are mundane, such as who does the dishes, who puts out the garbage and who writes the shopping list. Some are life-and-death, such as how childbirth and cancer treatment are done. Pam had been an activist in the women's movement over twenty years. We had been through the politics of dishwashing, among other things. She could see the gender politics in cancer medicine, and was not willing to be put down again.

The first tumour, which Pam discovered through routine screening, was so advanced that it required a mastectomy, surgical removal of the whole breast. This is a frightening (though not in itself life-threatening) operation which leaves a long scar where the breast had been. Recovering from the operation, Pam made contact with the support services available to mastectomy patients. It turned out that the main services provided were: supply of an artificial breast, in the appropriate size to replace the one that was lost; visits from women who came to give grooming and dress advice so that the patient could present a normal, attractive feminine appearance to the world; and advice on how to restore family normality, overcome a husband's (expected) sexual disgust at a mutilated body, and deal with children's anxiety about their mother's being taken away from them.

This, too, is political. It is about placing women back in the culture of heterosexual femininity. It is about denying that normality has been rent. It is about holding women responsible for other people's emotional needs. And – not least – it is about restoring normal services to men.

But this politics operates at so deep a level of emotion that it is hardly perceptible as politics unless one is already aware of gender issues. Many women dedicate their lives to making a family and seeing it through the life-cycle. A sense of having an attractive or at least presentable body is an important part of Australian culture's construction of womanhood. Women who are shocked by a major operation, and terrified by discovering they have a deadly disease, are unlikely to revolt against stereotyping, especially when it is presented to them as a form of care by other women.

Gender politics almost always has this dimension of intimacy, as well as involving larger social relations. That is one reason gender change can be so threatening, to many women as well as to many men. Impending changes can upset not only impersonal cultural or institutional arrangements. They also, at the same time and inseparably, upset people's cherished images of themselves, assumptions about personal relationships, their social embodiment and habits of everyday conduct.

Pam's experience was very close, for me; but the personal politics of gender is found everywhere, so I will give some examples from other parts of the world. One comes from Costa Rica in central America, and is narrated by Susan Mannon (2006). Costa Rica is a banana and coffee exporter, vulnerable to price fluctuations; the Latin American debt crisis of the 1980s drove the country into a neoliberal restructuring, in which many men became unemployed. Mannon interviewed middle-aged married people in an urban area, and tells particularly about one couple, called Cecilia and Antonio, who had lived through these events.

Their household had been set up on a breadwinner/housewife basis, though this was an anxious position as Antonio was an unskilled public sector worker. This gender division was not forced on Cecilia, she was an active participant in creating demarcations between family roles. Economic need drove change; as inflation gripped, Cecilia, like other married women, returned to the money economy. She did this at first by renting out a room in their house – in effect, commodifying her domestic work. In the 1990s the sharp breadwinner/housewife division began to blur – by Cecilia expanding her labour, not Antonio, who did not help around the house. He held on to authority in the family, with support from patriarchal norms in the society around; Cecilia did not use her new economic strength in bargaining with him. Too serious a challenge might have disrupted the social position of respectability that she was actually trying to protect. Patience and love won out.

In the Indian province of Andhra Pradesh there is a relatively high prevalence of HIV. This was recognized in the early 2000s and various public health initiatives have followed. A vigorous organizing project among local sex workers is Project Parivartan. Most are women who come from working-class, lower-caste positions who are marginal in society; gender inequalities are deeply entrenched and sex work itself is stigmatizing. The power differentials, therefore, are steep. This is reflected inside the sex trade, where it is usually the privilege of male clients to decide whether or not to use a condom.

A project report (George and Blankenship 2007) relates experiences of activists in Parivartan when trying to protect themselves from the epidemic by insisting on condom use. In one case, when a customer had solicited the worker on the street and paid in advance, she took him to a rented room, where he refused to use a condom. A dispute arose about the money; the customer eventually 'threatened to shout and wake the neighbours, and put the house owner to shame'. The threat was effective, because this would reveal the woman's sex work and disrupt the arrangements under which she earned her living. Even so elementary a change as introducing condom use involves struggle.

Chapter 2 described changes in conceptions of gender in Soviet and post-Soviet Russia. Anna Temkina (2008) reports a life-history study with middle-class women in St Petersburg that takes the story one step further. Different sexual 'scripts' can be distinguished in their stories. The women who had grown up in the Soviet period had lives organized by marriage, usually placed themselves in a passive position in their narratives, and described themselves as objects of men's desire – all reasonably in accord with Soviet gender ideology. In short, Temkina observes, their sexual lives were ruled by others and by the surrounding conditions.

But this is not the dominant story among younger women, who have grown up in the turmoil of the 1990s and under the new capitalist regime. These women describe themselves as having agency in their sexual lives, being more likely to emphasize seeking their own pleasure, or using their sexuality to gain benefits, i.e. bargaining with men. They are still under constraints. As the limited Soviet emancipation of women was rolled back, neo-traditionalist ideologies of gender emerged, and a new public patriarchy was constructed. But the young women of the 2000s are making more conscious choices about sexuality, contraception and relationships, being more inclined to see their lives as women as a project than as a destiny.

When the Women's Liberation movement said 'the personal is political', they were making a point that still holds good. There is a gender politics in our most intimate relationships and decisions. Struggles here are not susceptible to sweeping gestures; the complexities are many, the price of change can be high, and sometimes one just wants to forget it. But this intimate politics always underlies the more public politics and cannot be abandoned.

Public politics: movements and institutions

It used to be thought that political movements directly expressed an underlying interest or group identity, that they simply represented a class, a sex, a nation. Or if they didn't, they should – and would, once a little problem of false consciousness was fixed.

We now recognize more complexity in political processes, and recognize that language and symbolism are more than reflections – they construct identities and help create movements. Yet it would be as much a mistake to assume interests are *only* discursively constructed as it was to assume the opposite; this would be to privilege one dimension of social life over all the others. Movements in gender politics do in fact follow the broad outlines of social divisions and interests that are defined in power relations, economic relations and emotional relations, as well as in discourse. By and large, movements for change in patriarchal gender orders have arisen from women, or from marginalized groups of men; by and large, the defence of patriarchy has been undertaken by men and by relatively privileged women.

Historically the most important movement in gender politics has been feminism. I have said so much about this movement earlier in the book that I won't say more here. It is necessary to say that not all political movements among women are feminist. Raka Ray's (1999) study of women's politics in India gives a classic example. The Communist Party of India (Marxist), the long-term governing party in the province of West Bengal, established a women's organization called Paschim Banga Gana-tantrik Mahila Samiti. This functioned mainly to implement the official line coming down from the male leadership of the party – and that line insisted on solidarity between working-class women and men, not on the specific interests of women. Consequently the women of the Samiti, while working for women's economic and educational advance, shied away from anything that implied a direct challenge to men – for instance, from making a public issue of domestic violence, though that was a major issue for feminists all over India.

Of course this is not peculiar to India. Postwar Japan, for instance, saw a remarkable growth of women's organizations – women had gained the vote, and in the 1950s and 1960s were an important constituency. As Kazuko Tanaka (1977) describes, the men's parties set up women's auxiliaries to claim this constituency, and there were also big state-based women's organizations; the whole amounted to a large-scale organiza-tion of women. But these organizations were tied to a patriarchal politi-cal system. When Women's Liberation arrived, it represented a radical break. As in the United States and Europe, the claim for *autonomous* women's organization was a vital departure – and from that, the shape of modern gender politics has developed.

Gay Liberation, emerging in the United States at almost the same time, similarly involved autonomous organization, combining the personal and the structural. Public demonstrations produced similar feelings of exhilaration and common purpose. Lesbian and gay politics, however, involved another dimension, the process of 'coming out'. Making a decla-ration to oneself, one's family, one's friends and workmates can be dif-ficult and takes time. Adjustments and realignments in everyday life have to be made. The collective process of establishing a community, an iden-tity in the culture, and a presence in politics and economic life both depends on the individual process and supports it.

There was an extra complication in gay politics, because a gender division ran down the middle of it. Lesbians and gay men are not in the same social situation, or even the same political situation – laws that criminalized homosexual sex for men, in many countries, ignored women. So did some gay male activists. Gay Liberation itself was mainly a men's movement – though the iconic action with which it began, the 1969 'Stonewall' anti-police riot in New York, was led by transsexual and transvestite prostitutes. Tensions around the representation of women in homosexual politics have continued.

A decade after the emergence of Gay Liberation, homosexual men's politics was transformed by the HIV/AIDS epidemic. A whole new set of relationships, with doctors and the state, had to be negotiated, while a hostile symbolic politics about infection, pollution and uncleanness, whipped up by homophobic religious leaders, politicians and media, had to be dealt with. Both jobs had to be done in a context of illness, bereavement and fear. Gay communities in the metropole not only survived this terrible crisis, but evolved new responses and community education approaches, creating AIDS support organizations and the 'safe sex' strategy (Kippax, Connell, Dowsett and Crawford 1993). In poor countries, men who have sex with men (MSM, an awkward phrase that AIDS researchers and campaigners evolved to cover many different situations and identities) lack economic resources, and may also face homophobic governments. This is a serious problem in Africa, which has the highest burden of HIV infection and illness. Governments in Senegal and Zimbabwe, to name two, have made homosexual men targets for blame and persecution – which has disrupted AIDS prevention work.

Though there are some homophobic movements, what AIDS activists mainly came up against was not a movement, but an institutional structure that uses established authority to pursue gender politics. And this is also the main opposition that feminism has met.

There are explicitly anti-feminist movements, to be sure, such as the charmingly named 'Women Who Want to be Women' that once existed in the United States and 'REAL Women' that still exists in Canada. Small 'fathers' rights' groups who are fiercely hostile to feminism arise in many countries, and accuse divorce courts of being biassed against men. Anti-abortion movements, usually drawing on the membership of hard-line churches, have been the most successful anti-feminist campaigns of all, intimidating abortion providers, and eventually capturing control of many international aid programmes via the US government.

Even this, however, depended on right-wing control of the US state. The biggest force of resistance to women's reproductive rights internationally has been the Catholic church. As Mala Htun's (2003) study makes clear, church intransigence has prevented abortion reform right across Latin America in the last generation. (The entirely predictable outcome is that rich women can get safe abortion, poor women cannot.)

The defence of patriarchal gender orders has not, on the whole, required social movements among men. It has been accomplished by the normal functioning of the patriarchal institutions described in previous chapters – the state, the corporations, the media, the religious hierarchies. Certainly there is political intent: most mass media in the world are persistently anti-feminist, some of them (such as the Murdoch media empire) strikingly so. But for the most part, this political intent hardly needs to be articulated; everyday practice does the job.

Take, for example, military forces, which are easily recognized as patriarchal institutions. Frank Barrett (1996), researching gender patterns in US naval officer training, documents an oppressive but efficient regime emphasizing competition, physical hardness, conformity and a sense of elite membership. This is designed to produce a narrowly defined hegemonic masculinity, and therefore it creates serious problems for women trainees, since women began entering US military forces under 'equal opportunity' principles. The training works by linking the sense of personal worth to the needs of an organization that specializes in violence. Similar patterns are seen in Sinclair-Webb's (2000) account of military training in Turkey, already discussed; in Ruth Seifert's (1993) study of military training in Germany; and in other countries.

Not all men buy in to the defence of patriarchy. There is even resistance to military training where it is socially obligatory, as Sinclair-Webb shows. One of the most interesting forms of gender politics in the last generation has been the emergence of gender-equality movements among heterosexual men (called 'pro-feminist' men in the United States). Most of these movements are small, and local in their effects. Tina Sideris (2005) describes one that emerged in South Africa, where since the end of apartheid there has been a public principle of gender equality in tension with longstanding and often violent local patriarchies. Sideris describes interviews with a group of men in the rural Nkomazi region near the border with Mozambique, who are trying to move to a more respectful and gender-equal practice in their lives. All are married, with children. They are able to renegotiate the gender division of labour in their households, and adopt nonviolence. But they find it difficult to shift the meaning of masculinity away from being a head of household; in this gender regime, the authority dimension seems hardest to shift.

That is an informal movement; in other places gender-equality politics among men is more organized. For instance, I have read a *Trainer's Manual* produced by four non-government organizations in India, intended for change programmes among men and boys (SAHAJ 2005). This carefully designed resource includes modules on equality, on gender itself, on sexuality, health, violence and facilitation skills. It is highly practical, and obviously grows out of organizational experience in campaigns both with men and with women. Its coverage is reasonably like the syllabuses of educational programmes for boys and young men I have seen in other countries, including my own.

Finally, I should recall that gender politics also occurs in social movements that are not explicitly gender- or sexuality-based. Nina Laurie (2005) illustrates this in the 'water wars' in Cochabamba, Bolivia, in 1999–2000. In this famous struggle, a local mobilization overcame the attempt by a neoliberal national government and an international corporate consortium to privatize the water supplies. The leaders became international heroes. Laurie notes how the course of the struggle involved a contest between styles of masculinity, expressed in language and subjectivities – the neoliberal modernizer, the marginalized local engineer, the indigenous or mestizo organizer – with an unexpected outcome, the defeat of the transnational executives. Further back in history, the same point has often been made about the celebration of heroic masculinities and the marginalization of women in colonial liberation movements, in union movements and in ethnic identity movements.

The stakes: patriarchal dividend, gender harm and gender good

What is political about gender? In one of the foundation texts of Women's Liberation, *Sexual Politics*, Kate Millett (1972: 23) defined politics as 'power-structured relationships, arrangements whereby one group of persons is controlled by another'. What made her argument scandalous was that she applied this definition to the relation between women and men.

Power, as will be clear from the analysis in this book, is only one form of gender inequality. Inequalities exist across a range of resources, from income and wealth to social honour and cultural authority. Inequalities construct interests (whether or not the interests are articulated). Those benefiting from inequalities have an interest in defending them. Those who bear the costs have an interest in ending them.

Gender inequalities are usually expressed in terms of women's lack of resources relative to men's. For instance, chapter 1 cited statistics that show women's average incomes, world-wide, as about 56 per cent of men's. While this way of presenting information makes sense in establishing a case for reform, it continues the bad old habit of defining women by their relation to men. We should also turn the equation around and consider the surplus of resources made available to men. The same figures, read this way, show men's average incomes, world-wide, as 179 per cent of women's.

I call this surplus the *patriarchal dividend*: the advantage to men as a group from maintaining an unequal gender order. Money income is not the only kind of benefit. Others are authority, respect, service, safety, housing, access to institutional power, emotional support, and control over one's own life. The patriarchal dividend, of course, is reduced as overall gender equality grows.

It is important to note that the patriarchal dividend is the benefit to men *as a group*. Some men get more of it than others, other men get less, or none, depending on their location in the social order. A wealthy businessman draws large dividends from the gendered accumulation process in advanced capitalism. On a world scale, the dividends may be almost in the realm of fantasy – consider the fortunes of Bill Gates ($56 billion), Warren Buffett ($52 billion) and Carlos Slim Helú ($49 billion), the three richest humans in 2007. By contrast, an unemployed working-class man may draw no patriarchal dividend in an economic sense at all. Specific groups of men may be bluntly excluded from parts of the patriarchal dividend. Thus homosexual men, in most parts of the world, are excluded from the authority and respect attached to men who embody hegemonic forms of masculinity; though they may, and in rich countries often do, share men's general economic advantages.

Some women also participate in the patriarchal dividend, generally by being married to wealthy men. Such women draw from the gendered accumulation process, i.e. live on a profit stream generated in part by other women's underpaid and unpaid labour.

Considerable numbers of women in rich and even middle-income countries are able to benefit directly from other women doing the domestic labour in their households; very often, women from disadvantaged ethnic groups, such as Black or Latina women in the United States. A multi-lateral international trade in domestic work has now developed. For instance, very large numbers of Filipina women are now in domestic service in middle-class households in eastern and southern Asia, while other women travel from Moldava in eastern Europe to domestic service in Turkey (Chang and Ling 2000, Keough 2006). This transfer of domestic labour has allowed many middle-class women to move into professional or business careers, without putting pressure on middle-class *men* to raise their share of domestic labour.

The patriarchal dividend is the main stake in contemporary gender politics. Its scale makes patriarchy worth defending. The small band of sex-role reformers in the 1970s who attempted to persuade men that

Women's Liberation was good for them were undoubtedly right about the costs of hegemonic masculinity. But the same reformers hopelessly underestimated the patriarchal dividend. They missed what very large numbers of men stand to gain from current arrangements in terms of power, economic advantage, authority, peer respect, sexual access, and so on. Thus they missed the interest most men have in sustaining – and, where necessary, defending – the current gender order.

To argue that the current gender order should be changed is to claim that it does more harm than good. The harm of gender is first and foremost in the system of inequality in which women and girls are exploited, discredited and made vulnerable to abuse and attack. The still massive incidence of domestic violence, rape and child sexual abuse (mainly, though not exclusively, of girl children) is an easily recognized marker of power and vulnerability. In official discourse, such 'problems' are the actions of a minority of men out of control. But they would not occur on the scale they do unless violence and abuse were sustained by the interplay of many other mechanisms of the social order, which operate in the economic, cultural and emotional dimensions.

The harm of gender is also found in specific patterns in the gender order that are given power to affect the world by the collective resources of the society. Contemporary hegemonic masculinity, to take the most striking case, is dangerous, regardless of the patriarchal dividend. It is dangerous because it provides a cultural rationale for inter-personal violence, and because, in alliance with state and corporate power, it drives arms races, strip mining and deforestation, hostile labour relations and the abuse of technologies from motor transport to genetic engineering. It is harmful to men themselves; the masculinity reformers were on strong ground when they argued that men would be safer not fighting, would be healthier without competitive stress, and would have a better life with improved relations with women and children.

But if gender in these respects is harmful, it is in other respects a source of pleasure, creativity and other things we greatly value. Gender organizes our sexual relationships, which are sources of personal delight and growth; and our relations with children, which are sources of cultural delight and growth. Gender is integral to the cultural riches of most regions in the world, from *Noh* plays to reggae and hiphop. It is difficult to imagine Shakespeare's plays, Homer's *Iliad*, Joyce's *Ulysses*, Rumi's poetry, the *Ramayana*, or Bergman's films, without gender. The joys, tensions and complications of gender relations are among the most potent sources of cultural creation.

It is one of the most attractive features of recent queer politics that it has rediscovered the energy of gender practices, by shifting them off their conventional axes. Starting with the US direct action group Queer Nation in 1990, a great deal of creativeness has been unleashed in a variety of cultural forms. Pleasures in gender display, in erotic inventiveness, in alternative embodiments, in games with gender language, are very evident.

This pleasure and skill can be found in other spaces too. In the elementary schools studied by Barrie Thorne, for instance (chapter 2), there is no doubt that the children took pleasure in learning to do gender. The lifelong gender projects I defined in chapter 6 are not tales of woe; they are for great numbers of people complex and satisfying accomplishments. Moments where the integrity of a gender project is lost, moments of gender vertigo, can be extremely distressing experiences.

I would argue, then, that the stakes in gender politics include the value of gender as well as its harm. Gender politics has the possibility of shaping pleasures as well as distributing resources, and making possible a more creative culture.

The nature and purpose of gender politics

Given these possibilities, 'gender politics' has to be understood as more than an interest-group struggle over inequalities. In the most general sense, gender politics is about the *steering* of the gender order in history. It represents the struggle to have the endless re-creation of gender relations through practice turn out a particular way.

This definition includes the intimate politics of personal life as much as the large-scale politics of institutions. The making of the configurations of practice that we call 'masculinities' and 'femininities' has a political dimension, is a matter of social struggle. Consciousness-raising, formal education and therapy are among the benign forms. School and family discipline, confrontational policing, imprisonment are less benign but equally political, being applications of power intended to shape personality – and often calling out protest masculinity among working-class and ethnic minority boys and young men. Advertising and entertainment directed to children and youth are among the manipulative forms.

Though there have been stateless societies, and gender politics occurs in many other arenas, the state (both national and international) is the most important focus of gender politics in the contemporary world. Even in a neoliberal era, where the market is exalted and many public institutions are privatized, the state remains the most important steering mechanism in economies. And it has powerful steering capacities in other areas of life too, as the story of women's reproductive rights shows. The state has power to grant, or deny, recognition to groups, movements, institutions and individuals. State authority even makes an authoritative determination of an individual's position in the gender order – mine is stated on a birth certificate issued by the State of New South Wales – and either prevents, or sets rules for, changing that determination.

Therefore the state is not only the most important institutional player in gender politics, it is also the stake in a great deal of gender politics. Movements constantly try to influence how the state acts, or even to capture some part of state power, in order to steer the gender order in the direction they want. Women's parties have, so far, had little success in electoral politics. But women's movements as pressure groups or as elements in coalitions have had significant impacts; and at certain times gay rights movements have, too. When a Labor Party government replaced a conservative coalition in Australia in 2007, it undertook to reform laws and regulations that discriminated against lesbian and gay couples – for instance in tax, health and social security – and found more than 100 discriminatory measures in existence.

The significance of the state is very clear when we think about the involvement of heterosexual men in achieving gender equality. Without question, this has moved furthest in Scandinavia. The story is told in some detail in Øystein Holter's *Can Men Do It? Men and Gender Equality – The Nordic Experience* (2003). Only a few generations ago, the Nordic countries were socially conservative places with economies dominated by heavily masculinized industries – fishing, timber, mining – resulting in a stark gender division of labour. Gender relations have changed; Scandinavia now leads the world in women's representation in the public realm, men's involvement in child care, and other measures. The state's role in that change has been crucial; for instance, in providing economic support for fathers' involvement in the care of young children. Men do change, Holter argues, when the surrounding conditions allow it, and public policy can make the difference.

It is often clear what gender reform movements are fighting against – discriminatory laws, gender-based violence, social oppression. But what are they fighting for? What are the ultimate goals? Where do they want to steer society, in the long run?

Here there is a significant division, related to the discussion of inequality and gender harm in the previous section. Many feminists think that gender is inherently about inequality. In effect, they see the patriarchal dividend as the core of the gender order, and gender harm as unavoidable in any gender system. Logically, then, they see the goal of gender politics as the abolition of gender. As I remarked in chapter 5, this represents a conceivable 'end of history' for gender relations, where the reach of gender relations around the reproductive arena is reduced to zero.

An exceptionally clear statement of this view is offered by the US feminist Judith Lorber in *Breaking the Bowls: Degendering and Feminist Change* (2005). Recognizing that gender, however interwoven with other social structures, 'still exerts an enormous organizing, socializing and discriminatory power', Lorber sees two possible responses: acts of individual rebellion, or a strategy of de-gendering. She argues for de-gendering families, workplaces and politics; for seeking the abolition of gender wherever it is found; and for defining 'a world without gender' as the goal.

But there is another possibility. While de-gendering is a good tactic in many practical situations (for instance, those affected by anti-discrimination laws), as an ultimate goal it is extremely pessimistic. For it assumes there is a whole realm of human relations that cannot be democratized, and so must be abolished.

The real alternative to de-gendering, it seems to me, is a strategy of gender democracy. This strategy seeks to equalize gender orders, rather than shrink them to nothing. Conceptually, this assumes that gender does not, in itself, imply inequality. The fact that there are in the world gender orders with markedly different levels of inequality is some evidence in support.

That democratization is a possible strategy for a more just society is indicated by the many social struggles that have actually changed gender relations towards equality. The Nordic public policy regime just mentioned is a large-scale example; the intimate politics that has gone into producing the American 'fair families' described by Barbara Risman (1998) is another; the village-level economic changes catalyzed by Prince Thangkhiew in the Meghalaya hills (chapter 2) are a third.

A logic of gender democratization, rather than gender abolition, has some points to recommend it. It would be easier within this strategy to preserve what I called, in the previous section, gender good – the many pleasures, cultural riches, identities and other practices that arise in gender orders and that people value. It does not imply isolating the reproductive arena from social structures and institutions, but rather socially organizing the processes of conception, birth, baby care and child rearing on equal and inclusive lines. It connects the logic of gender reform with the ideals and practices of democratic struggle in other spheres of life. I don't think any strategy of gender reform will be easy – on that, everyone in the field will agree – but these look like significant advantages.

Gender politics on a world scale

Through this book I have emphasized, as contemporary gender analysis does, both the diversity of situations across the world and the global scope of gender issues. Chapter 7's analysis of the emerging global gender order suggests two transnational arenas of struggle for democratization: in global institutions and in the interactions between gender orders.

Democratization in the arena of global institutions is straightforward in concept though difficult in practice. It is the same kind of process as the democratization of institutions at the national or local level. In practical terms, it means such things as attempting to get equal employment opportunity in transnational corporations, ending the misogyny and homophobia in international media, gaining equal representation of women and men in international forums, ending gender discrimination in international labour markets, and creating anti-discrimination norms in the public culture.

A world-wide agency of change is already in existence. Feminist movements have a presence in international meetings (Stienstra 2000). This works to some extent through diplomatic delegations, and more consistently through the growing presence of non-government organizations. NGOs are now a recognized category of participants in United Nations activities and some are explicitly feminist. They interact with the women's units or programmes in international organizations such as UNESCO, and there is a certain amount of coordination of these activities through the UN Division for the Advancement of Women. There is also some international presence of gay and lesbian movements, particularly in human rights agencies and in the UN Global Programme on AIDS.

These forces have been able to place some issues about gender relations on the agendas of diplomacy and the international state. The United Nations set up a Commission on the Status of Women as early as 1946. Article 2 of the 1948 Universal Declaration of Human Rights banned discrimination on the basis of sex, as well as race, religion, etc. It has been followed by specific agreements about the rights of women, culminating in the Convention on the Elimination of All Forms of Discrimination against Women, introduced in 1979. The human rights agenda has been far more important than the 'men's movement' in winning support for gender equality from men in international organizations – support that has been vital in creating the spaces in which women's groups have operated.

The most important consequences of this pressure have been in development agendas. From the 1940s to the 1960s a global apparatus of development aid was created (both driven, and distorted, by Cold War politics). It was accepted early that improving the literacy, skills and knowledge of girls and women was a key move in development and 'modernization' (at a time when modernization was uncritically accepted as a goal). Consequently, in most parts of the world, a vast social investment was made in the elementary education of girls and in adult literacy programmes for rural and working-class women. Over time, this effort took on a gender-equality logic, and was pushed forward into secondary and higher education – where it is still active. One of the current UN Millennium Development goals, adopted in 2000, is to promote gender equality and empower women, with the specific target of eliminating gender disparities at all levels of education by 2015.

Alongside the education agenda, linked through the idea of improving human capital, was an economic aid agenda. Agencies such as the World Bank, as well as bilateral aid between governments of rich and poor countries, funded programmes to provide infrastructure, machinery, fertilizers, seeds (for the 'Green Revolution') and other means of economic growth. Before long it became obvious to feminists that not only were men in control of the aid programmes, most of the benefits went to men, and often women's lives were disrupted. The response was the 'Women in Development' agenda, which was pressed on aid agencies from the 1970s, to divert funds towards women in the recipient countries, and to recognize the consequences for women of existing development strategies.

In the 1990s a major debate occurred around this agenda. It was argued by some that a focus on women alone was ineffective; that men had to become change agents too if gender equality was to be achieved. A 'Gender and Development' strategy was proposed instead of 'Women in Development'. It was argued by others that bringing men into the only part of the global development agenda where women had actually consolidated power might reinforce patriarchy, not challenge it (White 2000, Chant and Gutmann 2002).

Similar debates were occurring in other arenas, as 'gender mainstreaming' ideas took hold in the European Union as well as the United Nations. It became important, therefore, to look at the specific role of men in gender equality processes. The issue was acknowledged in very general terms at the 1995 Beijing World Conference on Women. A more serious examination was launched in UN forums in the late 1990s and early 2000s. This culminated in a policy document 'The role of men and boys in achieving gender equality', adopted by the 2004 meeting of the UN Commission on the Status of Women: the first broad international agreement on this issue (Connell 2005). Over the next decade, we will see if it has an effect.

It is already clear that the forces pushing for gender democratization in global arenas are still weak in relation to the scale of the problem. They still have very little influence on transnational corporations and global markets. Obedience to anti-discrimination laws in head office does not prevent transnational corporations maintaining sharp gender divisions in their global workforce. Their characteristic search for cheap labour around the world often leads them, and their local suppliers, to exploit the weak industrial position of many women workers. This is especially the case where unions are hampered, or where governments have set up free-trade or special development zones to attract international capital (Marchand and Runyan 2000).

Even in the United Nations system, there is no unified force for change. The World Conferences on Women were vital in articulating world agendas for reform. But among the delegations attending were some from conservative Catholic governments, and some from conservative Muslim governments, actively opposed to gender equality. Therefore these conferences have seen sharp conflict over issues such as abortion, contraception and lesbianism. Even the concept of 'gender' was under attack at the 1995 Beijing conference, because it was supposed by right-wing forces to be a code word for feminism (Benden and Goetz 1998). Largely because of this conflict, the conferences have now ended.

Some of these divisions arise from the second dimension of global gender politics, the relations between gender orders. This is a more conceptually complex problem.

During the 1980s, divergences between the gender politics arising in different parts of the world were widely canvassed. The idea of 'third world feminism' emerged, contrasted with the feminism of the global metropole. While equality between women and men could be seen as a mark of modernity, it could also be seen as a sign of cultural imperialism. Forms of metropolitan feminism which emphasized women's autonomy aroused opposition from women who did not want to be separated from the men of their communities in struggles against racism, colonial or neo-colonial domination (Bulbeck 1988, Mohanty 1991).

Even conceptualizing a democratic agenda in this dimension is difficult. The interplay between gender orders arises historically from a system of global domination, that is, imperialism and colonialism. A democratic agenda must oppose the inequalities that have been inherited from this system, between global 'North' and global 'South'. This is a strong point made by those women who argue against separate political organization.

Yet the dilemma this leads to is troubling. The colonial system, and the globalized world economy, have certainly been run by men. But the anti-colonial struggle, too, was almost everywhere led by men. Post-colonial regimes have generally been patriarchal, and sometimes deeply misogynist or homophobic. In post-colonial regimes, the men of local elites have often been complicit with businessmen from the metropole in the exploitation of women's labour. Multinational corporations could not operate as they do without this cooperation. In places like the Philippines and Thailand, men of local elites have been central in the creation of international sex trade destinations. Arms trafficking similarly involves an interplay between the men who control local military forces and governments, and the men who run arms manufacturing corporations in the metropole.

The interplay between global structures and local gender orders certainly leads to change, but this is not a simple process. Sonia Montecino (2001), in a study of social diversity in Chile, writes of 'identities under tension'. Among women, for instance, a commitment to motherhood (often with religious undertones) remains strong. But in the new export-oriented economy, paid work is also becoming a basis of identity for middle-class women, rupturing the old symbolic meanings of gender. A similar observation is made by Dennis Altman (2001) about sexuality: the interplay with global capitalism has produced a range of novel identities, patterns of relationship, sexual communities and political processes. They belong neither to local nor to metropolitan cultures, but in a sense they belong to both – and more exactly, to the emerging global social order.

The forms of politics are also multiple. Feminists in the UN system are constrained by bureaucratic and diplomatic processes. The transnational feminist groups described by Valentine Moghadam in *Globalizing Women* (2005) generally reject bureaucracy and operate on an informal network basis. Even these groups are varied in structure and task: some focusing on trade and economic policy, some on solidarity work, some on contesting violence and social inequality.

Yet another layer of complexity is epistemological. The varied political movements around the world involve varied understandings of gender issues. In chapter 3, I adopted Bulbeck's argument that these are in some sense incommensurable; we cannot claim that any of them has an overriding claim to truth. In the context of gender politics, however, we cannot pause until we have resolved epistemological antinomies; we have to find practical ways of going on.

This is, more or less, what happens in human rights politics. Ambiguous general declarations, such as the Universal Declaration of Human Rights and the Convention on the Elimination of All Forms of Discrimination against Women, get read in different ways, but with enough overlap to allow many practical measures to be taken – each involving multi-lateral negotiations, and often conflicts.

Much the same is true of efforts at globalization from below by feminist movements in different parts of the world. Without exact agreement on concepts or even goals, enough overlap can be found to make practical action possible. In an essay called 'Transnational solidarity', Manisha Desai finds several common themes in women's resistance to neoliberal restructuring: asserting a right to work, struggling for a better quality of life, and nurturing nature. The book in which this essay appeared,

Women's Activism and Globalization (Naples and Desai 2002), collects many examples of women's organizing that reaches across borders. They show, however, a widespread problem; the links are most commonly South–North, i.e. between a group in a developing country and a group or agency from the metropole. Nevertheless, South–South relations are developing, and taking new forms, as shown by the World Social Forum, first held at Porto Alegre in Brazil in 2001. In gender politics, a notable example is the cooperation among Latin American feminist researchers that produced continent-wide statistics on the situation of women, and a sophisticated index of the level of achievement of gender equality (Valdés and Gomáriz 1995, Valdés 2001).

Let me add a final thought – my contribution to the layers of meaning. The criterion of democratic action in the world gender order must be what democracy always means: moving towards equality of participation, power and respect. In global spaces, this criterion applies at the same time to relations within any gender order and to relations between gender orders. Contradiction can't be avoided. The conflicts at the World Conferences for Women illustrate the point. Migratory domestic labour illustrates the point. The sex trade illustrates the point. The dilemmas of homosexual men under homophobic regimes illustrate the point. Yet progressive movements cannot evacuate these arenas simply because democratic practice is difficult. Anti-democratic forces are certainly not evacuating them.

As feminism has found, one cannot go global without being profoundly changed. Knowledge about gender has to be reconsidered again and again, in the light of the changing gender dynamics that appear in world gender politics. Given this willingness to learn, I am convinced that gender theory and research can play a significant role in making a more democratic world.

References

Achebe, Chinua. 1958. *Things Fall Apart*. London: Heinemann.

Adler, Alfred. [1927] 1992. *Understanding Human Nature*, trans. C. Brett. Oxford: Oneworld.

Alsop, Rachel, Annette Fitzsimons and Kathleen Lennon. 2002. *Theorizing Gender*. Cambridge: Polity.

Altman, Dennis. 1972. *Homosexual: Oppression and Liberation*. Sydney: Angus & Robertson.

2001. *Global Sex*. Chicago: University of Chicago Press.

Ampofo, Akosua Adomako, Josephine Beoku-Betts, Wairimu Ngaruiya Njambi and Mary Osirim. 2004. 'Women's and gender studies in English-speaking sub-Saharan Africa: a review of research in the social sciences', *Gender & Society* 18: 685–714.

Arnfred, Signe. 2003. 'African gender research: a view from the North', *CODES-RIA Bulletin*, 2003 no. 1: 6–9.

Arnot, Madeleine, Miriam David and Gaby Weiner. 1999. *Closing the Gender Gap: Postwar Education and Social Change*. Cambridge: Polity.

Bakare-Yusuf, Bibi. 2003. ' "Yorubas don't do gender": a critical review of Oyeronke Oyewumi's *The Invention of Women: Making an African Sense of Western Gender Discourses*'. *African Identities* 1: 121–43.

Balandier, Georges. [1955] 1970. *The Sociology of Black Africa: Social Dynamics in Central Africa*. London: André Deutsch.

Balme, Jane and Sandra Bowdler. 2006. 'Spear and digging stick: the origin of gender and its implications for the colonization of new continents', *Journal of Social Archaeology* 6, 3: 379–401.

Banner, Lois W. 1983. *American Beauty*. Chicago: University of Chicago Press.

Barbieri, Teresita de. 1992. 'Sobre la categoría genero. Una introducción teórico-metodologica' ['On the category of gender: a theoretical–methodological introduction'], *Revista Interamericana de Sociología* 6: 147–78.

Barrett, Frank J. 1996. 'Gender strategies of women naval officers', in *Women's Research and Education Institute: Conference on Women in Uniformed Services*. Washington, DC.

Bauer, Robin, Josch Hoenes and Volker Woltersdorff, eds. 2007. *Unbeschreiblich Männlich: Heteronormativitätskritische Perspektiven*. Hamburg: Männerschwarm.

Beauvoir, Simone de. [1949] 1972. *The Second Sex*. Harmondsworth: Penguin.

Bebel, August. [1879] 1971. *Women under Socialism [Die Frau und der Sozialismus]*. New York: Schocken Books.

Bell, Diane. 1983. *Daughters of the Dreaming*. Melbourne: McPhee Gribble, Allen & Unwin.

Bem, Sandra L. 1974. 'The measurement of psychological androgyny', *Journal of Consulting and Clinical Psychology* 42: 155–62.

Benden, Sally, and Anne-Marie Goetz. 1998. 'Who needs [sex] when you can have [gender]? Conflicting discourses on gender at Beijing', in *Feminist Visions of Development: Gender, Analysis and Policy*, ed. C. Jackson and R. Pearson. London: Routledge.

Bettencourt, B. Ann, and Norman Miller. 1996. 'Gender differences in aggression as a function of provocation: a meta-analysis', *Psychological Bulletin* 119: 422–7.

Bhaskaran, Suparna. 2004. *Made in India: Decolonizations, Queer Sexualities, Trans/national Projects*. New York: Palgrave Macmillan.

Blamires, Alcuin, ed. 1992. *Woman Defamed and Woman Defended: An Anthology of Medieval Texts*. Oxford: Clarendon Press.

Borchorst, Anette, and Birte Siim. 2002. 'The women-friendly welfare states revisited', *NORA* 10: 90–8.

Bottomley, Gillian. 1992. *From Another Place: Migration and the Politics of Culture*. Melbourne: Cambridge University Press.

Bulbeck, Chilla. 1988. *One World Women's Movement*. London: Pluto Press.
1997. *Living Feminism: The Impact of the Women's Movement on Three Generations of Australian Women*. Cambridge: Cambridge University Press.
1998. *Re-orienting Western Feminisms: Women's Diversity in a Postcolonial World*. Cambridge: Cambridge University Press.

Burton, Clare. 1987. 'Merit and gender: organisations and the mobilisation of masculine bias', *Australian Journal of Social Issues* 22: 424–35.

Butler, Judith. 1990. *Gender Trouble: Feminism and the Subversion of Identity*. New York: Routledge.

Califia, Patrick. 2003. *Sex Changes: The Politics of Transgenderism*. San Francisco: Cleis Press.

Caplan, Pat, ed. 1987. *The Cultural Construction of Sexuality*. London: Tavistock.

Chang, Kimberly A., and L. H. M. Ling. 2000. 'Globalization and its intimate other: Filipina domestic workers in Hong Kong', pp. 27–43 in Marianne H. Marchand and Anne Sisson Runyan, eds., *Gender and Global Restructuring*. London: Routledge.

Chant, Sylvia, and Matthew C. Gutmann. 2002. '"Men-streaming" gender? Questions for gender and development policy in the twenty-first century', *Progress in Development Studies* 2: 269–82.

Chapkis, Wendy. 1997. *Live Sex Acts: Women Performing Erotic Labor*. New York: Routledge.

Chiland, Colette. 2003. *Transsexualism: Illusion and Reality*. London: Continuum.

Chodorow, Nancy. 1978. *The Reproduction of Mothering: Psychoanalysis and the Sociology of Gender*. Berkeley: University of California Press.

1994. *Femininities, Masculinities, Sexualities: Freud and Beyond*. Lexington, Ky.: University Press of Kentucky.

Chopra, Radhika, ed. 2007. *Reframing Masculinities: Narrating the Supportive Practices of Men*. New Delhi: Orient Longman Private.

Cockburn, Cynthia. 1983. *Brothers: Male Dominance and Technological Change*. London: Pluto Press.

Collinson, David, David Knights and Margaret Collinson. 1990. *Managing to Discriminate*. London: Routledge.

Comte, Auguste. [1851–4] 1875–7. *System of Positive Polity, or, Treatise on Sociology*. London: Longman, Green.

Connell, Raewyn. 1987. *Gender and Power: Society, the Person and Sexual Politics*. Cambridge: Polity.

1995. *Masculinities*. Cambridge: Polity.

2000. *The Men and the Boys*. Cambridge: Polity.

2005. 'Change among the gatekeepers: men, masculinities, and gender equality in the global arena', *Signs* 30: 1801–25.

2006. 'Glass ceilings or gendered institutions? Mapping the gender regimes of public sector worksites', *Public Administration Review* 66: 837–49.

2007. *Southern Theory: The Global Dynamics of Knowledge in Social Science*. Cambridge: Polity.

Connell, R., and James W. Messerschmidt. 2005. 'Hegemonic masculinity: rethinking the concept', *Gender and Society* 19: 829–59.

Connell, R., T. Schofield, L. Walker et al. 1999. *Men's Health: A Research Agenda and Background Report*. Canberra: Commonwealth Department of Health and Aged Care.

Connell, R., and Julian Wood. 2005. 'Globalization and business masculinities', *Men and Masculinities* 7: 347–64.

Cummings, Katherine. 1992. *Katherine's Diary: The Story of a Transsexual*. Melbourne: Heinemann.

Cupples, Julie. 2005. 'Love and money in an age of neoliberalism: gender, work, and single motherhood in postrevolutionary Nicaragua', *Environment and Planning A*, 37: 305–22.

Daly, Mary. 1978. *Gyn/Ecology: The Metaethics of Radical Feminism*. Boston: Beacon Press.

Darwin, Charles. [1859] 1928. *The Origin of Species*. London: Dent.

Das, Veena. 1995. *Critical Events: An Anthropological Perspective on Contemporary India*. New Delhi: Oxford University Press.

Davidoff, Leonore, and Catherine Hall. 1987. *Family Fortunes: Men & Women of the English Middle Class 1780–1850*. London: Hutchinson.

Davies, Bronwyn. 1993. *Shards of Glass: Children Reading and Writing beyond Gendered Identities*. Sydney: Allen & Unwin.

Degler, Carl N. 1990. 'Darwinians confront gender: or, there is more to it than history', pp. 33–45 in D. L. Rhode, ed., *Theoretical Perspectives or Sexual Difference*. New Haven: Yale University Press.

Delphy, Christine. 1970. 'The main enemy'. Translated in *Close to Home: A Materialist Analysis of Women's Oppression*. London: Hutchinson.

1984. *Close to Home: A Materialist Analysis of Women's Oppression*. London: Hutchinson.

Derrida, Jacques. [1967] 1976. *Of Grammatology*. Baltimore: Johns Hopkins University Press.

Donaldson, Mike. 1991. *Time of our Lives: Labour and Love in the Working Class*. Sydney: Allen & Unwin.

Donaldson, Mike, and Scott Poynting. 2007. *Ruling Class Men: Money, Sex, Power*. Bern: Peter Lang.

Dowsett, Gary W. 1996. *Practicing Desire: Homosexual Sex in the Era of AIDS*. Stanford, Calif.: Stanford University Press.

2003. 'Some considerations on sexuality and gender in the context of AIDS', *Reproductive Health Matters* 11: 21–9.

Dull, Diana, and Candace West. 1991. 'Accounting for cosmetic surgery: the accomplishment of gender', *Social Problems* 38: 54–70.

Dunne, Gillian A. 1997. *Lesbian Lifestyles: Women's Work and the Politics of Sexuality*. Basingstoke: Macmillan.

Eagly, Alice H. 1987. *Sex Differences in Social Behavior: A Social-Role Interpretation*. Hillside, NJ: Lawrence Erlbaum.

Eisenstein, Hester. 1996. *Inside Agitators: Australian Femocrats and the State*. Sydney: Allen & Unwin.

Ellis, Havelock. 1928. *Studies in the Psychology of Sex*, vol. VII: *Eonism and other Supplementary Studies*. Philadelphia: F. A. Davis.

Engels, Friedrich. [1884] 1970. *The Origin of The Family, Private Property and the State*, pp. 191–334 in *Marx/Engels Selected Works*. Moscow: Progress Publishers.

Enloe, Cynthia. 1990. *Bananas, Beaches and Bases: Making Feminist Sense of International Politics*. Berkeley: University of California Press.

Epstein, Cynthia Fuchs. 1988. *Deceptive Distinctions: Sex, Gender and the Social Order*. New Haven: Yale University Press.

2007. 'Great divides: the cultural, cognitive, and social bases of the global subordination of women', *American Sociological Review* 72: 1–22.

Erikson, Erik H. 1950. *Childhood and Society*. London: Imago.

Essen, Mineke van. 2000. 'Gender in beweging: over pedagogiek en sekse in de Lichamelijke Opvoeding van de Twintigste EEUW', *Tijdschrift voor Genderstudies* 3: 25–35.

Fairweather, Hugh. 1976. 'Sex differences in cognition', *Cognition* 4: 231–80.

Fausto-Sterling, Anne. 2000. *Sexing the Body: Gender Politics and the Construction of Sexuality*. New York: Basic Books.

Ferguson, Ann Arnett. 2000. *Bad Boys: Public Schools in the Making of Black Masculinity*. Ann Arbor: University of Michigan Press.

Firestone, Shulamith. 1971. *The Dialectic of Sex*. London: Paladin.

Foley, Douglas. 1990. *Learning Capitalist Culture: Deep in the Heart of Tejas*. Philadelphia: University of Pennsylvania Press.

Foucault, Michel. 1977. *Discipline and Punish: The Birth of the Prison*, trans. A. Sheridan. New York: Pantheon.

Fox, Loren. 2003. *Enron: The Rise and Fall*. Hoboken: Wiley.

Franzway, Suzanne. 2000. *Sexual Politics and Greedy Institutions*. Sydney: Pluto Press.

Fraser, Nancy. 1989. *Unruly Practices: Power, Discourse and Gender in Contemporary Social Theory*. Cambridge: Polity, and Minneapolis: University of Minnesota Press.

Fregoso, Rosa Linda. 1993. *The Bronze Screen: Chicana and Chicano Film Culture*. Minneapolis: University of Minnesota Press.

Freud, Sigmund. [1900] 1953. *The Interpretation of Dreams*, in *Complete Psychological Works*, vols. IV–V. London: Hogarth.

[1905] 1953. *Three Essays on the Theory of Sexuality*, in *Complete Psychological Works*, vol. VII. London: Hogarth.

[1911] 1958. 'Psycho-analytic notes on an autobiographical account of a case of paranoia (dementia paranoides)', in *Complete Psychological Works*, vol. XII. London: Hogarth.

[1930] 1961. *Civilization and its Discontents*, in *Complete Psychological Works*, vol. XXI. London: Hogarth.

Frosh, Stephen, Ann Phoenix and Rob Pattman. 2002. *Young Masculinities: Understanding Boys in Contemporary Society*. Basingstoke: Palgrave.

Garber, Marjorie. 1992. *Vested Interests: Cross-Dressing and Cultural Anxiety*. New York: Routledge.

García Canclini, Néstor. 1999. *La globalización imaginada*. Buenos Aires: Paidós.

Gauthier, Xavière. 1981. 'Is there such a thing as women's writing?', pp. 161–4 in Elaine Marks and Isabelle de Courtivron, eds., *New French Feminisms: An Anthology*. London: Harvester.

Geary, David C. 1998. *Male, Female: The Evolution of Human Sex Differences*. Washington, DC: American Psychological Association.

George, Annie, and Kim Blankenship. 2007. 'Challenging masculine privilege: an unintended outcome of HIV prevention and sex worker empowerment interventions'. Paper presented at 'Politicising Masculinities: Beyond the Personal' conference, Dakar, October 2007.

Gherardi, Silva, and Barbara Poggio. 2001. 'Creating and recreating gender order in organizations', *Journal of World Business* 36: 245–59.

Ghoussoub, Mai. 2000. 'Chewing gum, insatiable women and foreign enemies: male fears and the Arab media', pp. 227–35 in Mai Ghoussoub and Emma Sinclair-Webb, eds., *Imagined Masculinities: Male Identity and Culture in the Modern Middle East*. London: Saqi Books.

Ghoussoub, Mai, and Emma Sinclair-Webb, eds., 2000. *Imagined Masculinities: Male Identity and Culture in the Modern Middle East*. London: Saqi Books.

Gierycz, Dorota. 1999. 'Women in decision-making: can we change the status quo?', pp. 19–30 in I. Breines, D. Gierycz and B. A. Reardon, eds., *Towards a Woman's Agenda for a Culture of Peace*. Paris: UNESCO.

Gilligan, Carol. 1982. *In a Different Voice: Psychological Theory and Women's Development*. Cambridge, Mass.: Harvard University Press.

Glass Ceiling Commission. 1995. *A Solid Investment: Making Full Use of the Nation's Human Capital. Recommendations*. Washington, DC: Federal Glass Ceiling Commission.

Glucksmann, Miriam [writing as Ruth Cavendish]. 1982. *Women on the Line*. London: Routledge & Kegan Paul.

Glucksmann, Miriam. 1990. *Women Assemble: Women Workers and the New Industries in Inter-war Britain*. London: Routledge.

—— 2000. *Cottons and Casuals: The Gendered Organisation of Labour in Time and Space*. Durham: sociologypress.

Goldberg, Steven. 1993. *Why Men Rule: A Theory of Male Dominance*. Chicago: Open Court.

Grosz, Elizabeth. 1994. *Volatile Bodies: Towards a Corporeal Feminism*. Sydney: Allen & Unwin.

Gutmann, Matthew C., ed. 2001. 'Men and Masculinities in Latin America'. Special issue of *Men and Masculinities* 3, 3.

Gutmann, Matthew C., and Mara Viveros Vigoya. 2005. 'Masculinities in Latin America', pp. 114–28 in Michael S. Kimmel, Jeff Hearn and Raewyn Connell, eds., *Handbook of Studies on Men & Masculinities*. Thousand Oaks: Sage.

Habermas, Jürgen. 1976. *Legitimation Crisis*. London: Heinemann.

Hacker, Helen Mayer. 1957. 'The new burdens of masculinity', *Marriage and Family Living* 19: 227–33.

Hagemann-White, Carol. 1987. 'Gendered modes of behavior – a sociological strategy for empirical research'. Paper presented at 3rd International Interdisciplinary Congress on Women, Dublin, July 1987. Published by Berliner Institut für Sozialforschung und Sozialwissenschaftliche Praxis.

—— 1992. *Strategien gegen Gewalt im Geschlechterverhältnis: Bestandsanalyse und Perspektiven*. Pffafenweiler: Centaurus-Verlagsgesellschaft.

Halpern, Diane F., and Mary L. LaMay. 2000. 'The smarter sex: a critical review of sex differences in intelligence', *Educational Psychology Review* 12: 229–46.

Harding, Sandra. 1986. *The Science Question in Feminism*. Ithaca, NY: Cornell University Press.

Harper, Catherine. 2007. *Intersex*. Oxford: Berg.

Herdt, Gilbert H. 1981. *Guardians of the Flutes: Idioms of Masculinity*. New York: McGraw-Hill.

Hill Collins, Patricia. 1991. *Black Feminist Thought: Knowledge, Consciousness, and the Politics of Empowerment*. New York: Routledge.

Hochschild, Arlie Russell. 1983. *The Managed Heart: Commercialization of Human Feeling*. Berkeley: University of California Press.

Hocquenghem, Guy. [1972] 1978. *Homosexual Desire*, trans. D. Dangoor. London: Allison & Busby.

Holland, Dorothy C., and Margaret A. Eisenhart. 1990. *Educated in Romance: Women, Achievement, and College Culture*. Chicago: University of Chicago Press.

Hollway, Wendy. 1994. 'Separation, integration and difference: contradictions in a gender regime', pp. 247–69 in H. L. Radtke and J. S. Henderikus, eds., *Power/Gender*. London: Sage.

Holter, Øystein Gullvåg. 2003. *Can Men Do It? Men and Gender Equality – the Nordic Experience*. Copenhagen: Nordic Council of Ministers.

——— 2005. 'Social theories for researching men and masculinities: direct gender hierarchy and structural inequality', pp. 15–34 in Michael S. Kimmel, Jeff Hearn and Raewyn Connell, eds., *Handbook of Studies on Men and Masculinities*. Thousand Oaks: Sage.

hooks, bell. 1984. *Feminist Theory: From Margin to Center*. Boston: South End Press.

Hooper, Charlotte. 2000. 'Masculinities in transition: the case of globalization', pp. 59–73 in Marianne H. Marchand and Anne Sisson Runyan, eds., *Gender and Global Restructuring*. London: Routledge.

Hountondji, Paulin J. 1997. 'Introduction: recentring Africa', pp. 1–39 in Paulin J. Hountondji, ed., *Endogenous Knowledge: Research Trails*. Dakar: CODESRIA.

Htun, Mala. 2003. *Sex and the State: Abortion, Divorce, and the Family under Latin American Dictatorships and Democracies*. Cambridge: Cambridge University Press.

Hyde, Janet Shibley. 1984. 'How large are gender-differences in aggression? A developmental meta-analysis', *Developmental Psychology* 20: 722–36.

——— 2005. 'The gender similarities hypothesis', *American Psychologist* 60, 6: 581–92.

Hyde, Janet Shibley, and Nita M. McKinley. 1997. 'Gender differences in cognition: results from meta-analyses', pp. 30–51 in P. J. Caplan, M. Crawford, J. S. Hyde and J. T. E. Richardson, eds., *Gender Differences in Human Cognition*. New York: Oxford University Press.

Inter-Parliamentary Union. 2007. 'Women in national parliaments', www.ipu.org/wmn-e/world.htm.

Irigaray, Luce. [1977] 1985. *This Sex Which is Not One*, trans. C. Porter and C. Burke. Ithaca, NY: Cornell University Press.

Jackson, Peter A. 1997. '*Kathoey*><gay><man: the historical emergence of gay male identity in Thailand', pp. 166–90 in L. Manderson and M. Jolly, eds., *Sites of Desire, Economies of Pleasure*. Chicago: University of Chicago Press.

Jaffee, Sara, and Janet Shibley Hyde. 2000. 'Gender differences in moral orientation: a meta-analysis', *Psychological Bulletin* 126: 703–26.

Jeffords, Susan. 1989. *The Remasculinization of America: Gender and the Vietnam War*. Bloomington: Indiana University Press.

Johnson, Pauline. 1994. *Feminism as Radical Humanism*. Sydney: Allen & Unwin.

Kanter, Rosabeth. 1977. *Men and Women of the Corporation*. New York: Basic Books.

Kartini. 2005. *On Feminism and Nationalism: Kartini's Letters to Stella Zeehandelaar, 1899–1903*. Clayton: Monash University Press.

Kemper, Theodore D. 1990. *Social Structure and Testosterone: Explorations of the Socio-bio-social Chain*. New Brunswick: Rutgers University Press.

Keough, Leyla J. 2006. 'Globalizing "postsocialism": mobile mothers and neoliberalism on the margins of Europe', *Anthropological Quarterly* 79: 431–61.

Kim, Nadia Y. 2006. ' "Patriarchy is so third world": Korean immigrant women and "migrating" white western masculinity', *Social Problems* 53: 519–36.

King, Dave. 1981. 'Gender confusions: psychological and psychiatric conceptions of transvestism and transsexualism', pp. 155–83 in Kenneth Plummer, ed., *The Making of the Modern Homosexual*. London: Hutchinson.

Kippax, Susan, Raewyn Connell, Gary W. Dowsett and June Crawford. 1993. *Sustaining Safe Sex: Gay Communities Respond to AIDS*. London: Falmer Press.

Kirk, David. 1993. *The Body, Schooling and Culture*. Geelong, Victoria: Deakin University Press.

Klein, Alan M. 1993. *Little Big Men: Bodybuilding Subculture and Gender Construction*. Albany, NY: State University of New York Press.

Klein, Viola. 1946. *The Feminine Character: History of an Ideology*. London: Kegan Paul, Trench, Trubner & Co.

Kling, Kristen, Janet Shibley Hyde, Caroline J. Showers and Brenda N. Buswell. 1999. 'Gender differences in self-esteem: a meta-analysis', *Psychological Bulletin* 125: 470–500.

Kollontai, Alexandra. 1977. *Selected Writings*, trans. A. Holt. London: Allison & Busby.

Komarovsky, Mirra. 1946. 'Cultural contradictions and sex roles', *American Journal of Sociology* 52: 184–9.

Kondo, Dorinne. 1999. 'Fabricating masculinity: gender, race, and nation in a transnational frame', pp. 296–319 in Caren Kaplan, Norma Alarcón and Minoo Moallem, eds., *Between Woman and Nation: Nationalisms, Transnational Feminisms, and the State*. Durham, NC: Duke University Press.

Krafft-Ebing, Richard von. [1886] 1965. *Psychopathia Sexualis*, 12th edition. New York: Paperback Library.

Kristeva, Julia. [1974] 1984. *Revolution in Poetic Language*. New York: Columbia University Press.

Laplanche, J., and J.-B. Pontalis. 1973. *The Language of Psycho-Analysis*. New York: Norton.

Laqueur, Thomas Walter. 1990. *Making Sex: Body and Gender from the Greeks to Freud*. Cambridge, Mass.: Harvard University Press.

Laurie, Nina. 2005. 'Establishing development orthodoxy: negotiating masculinities in the water sector', *Development and Change* 36: 527–49.

Lees, Sue. 1986. *Losing Out: Sexuality and Adolescent Girls*. London: Hutchinson.

Lenz, Ilse, Anja Szypulski and Beate Molsich, eds. 1996. *Frauenbewegungen International: Eine Arbeitsbibliographie*. Opladen: Leske & Budrich.

Lessing, Doris. 1962. *The Golden Notebook*. London: Michael Joseph.

Levin, Peter. 2001. 'Gendering the market: temporality, work, and gender on a national futures exchange', *Work and Occupations* 28: 112–30.

Lloyd, Moya. 2007. *Judith Butler: From Norms to Politics*. Cambridge: Polity, 2007.

Lorber, Judith. 2005. *Breaking the Bowls: Degendering and Feminist Change*. New York: Norton.

Luttrell, Wendy. 1997. *Schoolsmart and Motherwise: Working-Class Women's Identity and Schooling*. New York: Routledge.

Mac an Ghaill, Máirtín. 1994. *The Making of Men: Masculinities, Sexualities and Schooling*. Milton Keynes: Open University Press.

Maccoby, Eleanor E., ed. 1966. *The Development of Sex Differences*. Stanford, Calif.: Stanford University Press.

Maccoby, Eleanor E., and Carol Nagy Jacklin. 1975. *The Psychology of Sex Differences*. Stanford, Calif.: Stanford University Press.

Mackenzie, John M. 1987. 'The imperial pioneer and hunter and the British masculine stereotype in late Victorian and Edwardian times', pp. 176–98 in J. A. Mangan and James Walvin, eds., *Manliness and Morality: Middle-Class Masculinity in Britain and America, 1800–1940*. Manchester: Manchester University Press.

MacKinnon, Catharine A. 1983. 'Feminism, Marxism, method and the state: towards feminist jurisprudence', *Signs* 8: 635–58.

1989. *Toward a Feminist Theory of the State*. Cambridge, Mass.: Harvard University Press.

Mahalik, James R., Benjamin D. Locke, Larry H. Ludlow et al. 2003. 'Development of the conformity to masculine norms inventory', *Psychology of Men and Masculinity* 4: 3–25.

Malos, Ellen, ed. 1980. *The Politics of Housework*. London: Allison & Busby.

Mane, Purnima, and Peter Aggleton. 2001. 'Gender and HIV/AIDS: what do men have to do with it?' *Current Sociology* 49: 23–37.

Mannon, Susan E. 2006. 'Love in the time of neo-liberalism: gender, work, and power in a Costa Rican marriage', *Gender & Society* 20: 511–30.

Marchand, Marianne H., and Anne Sisson Runyan, eds. 2000. *Gender and Global Restructuring: Sightings, Sites and Resistances*. London: Routledge.

Martin, Patricia Yancey. 2006. 'Practising gender at work: further thoughts on reflexivity', *Gender, Work & Organization*, 13: 254–76.

Mead, Margaret. [1935] 1963. *Sex and Temperament in Three Primitive Societies*. New York: William Morrow.

Meekosha, Helen. 2006. 'What the hell are you? An intercategorical analysis of race, ethnicity, gender and disability in the Australian body politic', *Scandinavian Journal of Disability Research* 8: 161–76.

Melville, Herman. [1853] 1969. 'Bartleby the Scrivener', pp. 159–90 in D. J. Burrows and F. R. Lapides, eds., *Alienation: A Casebook*. New York: Crowell.

Menon, Nivedita, ed. 1999. *Gender and Politics in India*. New Delhi: Oxford University Press.

Menzies, Jackie, ed. 1998. *Modern Boy Modern Girl: Modernity in Japanese Art 1910–1935*. Sydney: Art Gallery of New South Wales.

Messerschmidt, James W. 1993. *Masculinities and Crime: Critique and Reconceptualization of Theory*. Lanham, Md.: Rowman & Littlefield.

1997. *Crime as Structured Action: Gender, Race, Class and Crime in the Making*. Thousand Oaks, Calif.: Sage.

Messner, Michael A. 2007. *Out of Play: Critical Essays on Gender and Sport*. Albany: State University of New York Press.

Midgley, Clare, ed. 1998. *Gender and Imperialism*. New York: St Martin's Press.

Mies, Maria. 1986. *Patriarchy and Accumulation on a World Scale: Women in the International Division of Labour*. London: Zed Books.

Mill, John Stuart. [1869] 1912. *The Subjection of Women*, in *J. S. Mill: Three Essays*. London: Oxford University Press.

Miller, Pavla. 1998. *Transformations of Patriarchy in the West, 1500–1900*. Bloomington: Indiana University Press.

Millett, Kate. 1972. *Sexual Politics*. London: Abacus.

Mills, Albert J., and Peta Tancred, eds. 1992. *Gendering Organizational Analysis*. Newbury Park, Calif.: Sage.

Mitchell, Juliet. 1966. 'Women: the longest revolution', *New Left Review* 40: 11–37.

1971. *Woman's Estate*. Harmondsworth: Penguin.

1974. *Psychoanalysis and Feminism*. New York: Pantheon Books.

Moghadam, Valentine M. 2005. *Globalizing Women: Transnational Feminist Networks*. Baltimore: Johns Hopkins University Press.

Mohanty, Chandra Talpade. 1991. 'Under Western eyes: feminist scholarship and colonial discourses', pp. 51–80 in C. T. Mohanty, A. Russo and L. Torres, eds., *Third World Women and the Politics of Feminism*. Bloomington: Indiana University Press.

2003. *Feminism Without Borders: Decolonizing Theory, Practicing Solidarity*. Durham, NC: Duke University Press.

Mohwald, Ulrich. 2002. *Changing Attitudes towards Gender Equality in Japan and Germany*. Munich: Iudicium.

Montecino, Sonia. 2001. 'Identidades y diversidades en Chile', pp. 65–98 in Manuel Antonio Garretón, ed., *Cultura y desarrollo en Chile*. Santiago: Andres Bello.

Moodie, T. Dunbar, with Vivienne Ndatshe. 1994. *Going for Gold: Men, Mines and Migration*. Johannesburg: Witwatersrand University Press.

Morgan, Robin, ed. 1970. *Sisterhood is Powerful: An Anthology of Writings from the Women's Liberation Movement*. New York: Vintage.

1984. *Sisterhood is Global: The International Women's Movement Anthology*. Garden City, NY: Anchor.

Morrell, Robert. 2001a. *From Boys to Gentlemen: Settler Masculinity in Colonial Natal 1880–1920*. Pretoria: University of South Africa.

ed. 2001b. *Changing Men in Southern Africa*. London: Zed Books.

Mudimbe, V. Y. 1994. *The Idea of Africa*. Bloomington: Indiana University Press.

Namaste, Viviane K. 2000. *Invisible Lives: The Erasure of Transsexual and Transgendered People*. Chicago: University of Chicago Press.

Nandy, Ashis. 1983. *The Intimate Enemy: Loss and Recovery of Self under Colonialism*. Delhi: Oxford University Press.

1987. *Traditions, Tyranny and Utopias: Essays in the Politics of Awareness*. New Delhi: Oxford University Press.

Naples, Nancy, and Manisha Desai, eds. 2002. *Women's Activism and Globalization: Linking Local Struggles and Transnational Politics*. New York: Routledge.

Newman, Meredith A., Robert A. Jackson and Douglas D. Baker. 2003. 'Sexual harassment in the federal workplace', *Public Administration Review* 63: 472–83.

Nilsson, Arne. 1998. 'Creating their own private and public: the male homosexual life space in a Nordic city during high modernity', *Journal of Homosexuality* 35: 81–116.

Novikova, Irina. 2000. 'Soviet and post-Soviet masculinities: after men's wars in women's memories', pp. 117–29 in I. Breines, R. Connell and I. Eide, eds., *Male Roles, Masculinities and Violence: A Culture of Peace Perspective*. Paris: UNESCO Publishing.

O'Connor, Julia S., Ann Shola Orloff and Sheila Shaver. 1999. *States, Markets, Families: Gender, Liberalism and Social Policy in Australia, Canada, Great Britain and the United States*. Cambridge: Cambridge University Press.

Odih, Pamela. 2007. *Gender and Work in Capitalist Economies*. Maidenhead: Open University Press.

Oetomo, Dede. 1996. 'Gender and sexual orientation in Indonesia', pp. 259–69 in L. J. Sears, ed., *Fantasizing the Feminine in Indonesia*. Durham, NC: Duke University Press.

Okeke-Ihejirika, Philomina E., and Susan Franceschet. 2002. 'Democratisation and state feminism: gender politics in Africa and Latin America', *Development and Change* 33: 439–66.

Oyéwùmí, Oyèrónké. 1997. *The Invention of Women: Making an African Sense of Western Gender Discourses*. Minneapolis: University of Minnesota Press.

Paap, Kris. 2006. *Working Construction: Why White Working Class Men Put Themselves – and the Labor Movement – In Harm's Way*. Ithaca: Cornell University Press.

Parker, Richard G. 1991. *Bodies, Pleasures and Passions: Sexual Culture in Contemporary Brazil*. Boston: Beacon Press.

Parsons, Talcott, and Robert F. Bales. 1956. *Family Socialization and Interaction Process*. London: Routledge & Kegan Paul.

Perkins, Roberta. 1983. *The 'Drag Queen' Scene: Transsexuals in Kings Cross*. Sydney: Allen & Unwin.

Peteet, Julie. 1994. 'Male gender and rituals of resistance in the Palestinian intifada: a cultural politics of violence', *American Ethnologist* 21: 31–49.

Peterson, Spike. 2003. *A Critical Rewriting of Global Political Economy: Integrating Reproductive, Productive and Virtual Economies*. London: Routledge.

Pfau-Effinger, Birgit. 1998. 'Gender cultures and the gender arrangement – a theoretical framework for cross-national research', *Innovation* 11: 147–66.

Pizan, Christine de. [1405] 1983. *The Book of the City of Ladies*. London: Pan Books.

Pleck, J. H., and J. Sawyer, eds. 1974. *Men and Masculinity*. Englewood Cliffs, NJ: Prentice-Hall.

Poster, Winifred R. 2002. 'Racialism, sexuality, and masculinity: gendering "global ethnography" of the workplace', *Social Politics* 9: 126–58.

Pringle, Rosemary. 1989. *Secretaries Talk: Sexuality, Power and Work*. Sydney: Allen & Unwin.

——— 1992. 'Absolute sex? Unpacking the sexuality/gender relationship', pp. 76–101 in R. Connell and G. W. Dowsett, eds., *Rethinking Sex: Social Theory and Sexuality Research*. Melbourne: Melbourne University Press.

Radcliffe, Sarah A., Nina Laurie and Robert Andolina. 2004. 'The transnationalization of gender and reimagining Andean indigenous development', *Signs* 29: 387–416.

Ray, Raka. 1999. *Fields of Protest: Women's Movements in India*. Minneapolis: University of Minnesota Press.

Reiter, Rayna Rapp. 1977. 'The search for origins: unravelling the threads of gender hierarchy', *Critique of Anthropology* 9 & 10: 5–24.

Reynolds, Robert. 2002. *From Camp to Queer: Re-making the Australian Homosexual*. Melbourne: Melbourne University Press.

Rigi, Jakob. 2003. 'The conditions of post-Soviet dispossessed youth and work in Almaty, Kazakhstan', *Critique of Anthropology*, 23: 35–49.

Risman, Barbara J. 1986. 'Can men "mother"? Life as a single father', *Family Relations* 35: 95–102.

——— 1998. *Gender Vertigo: American Families in Transition*. New Haven: Yale University Press.

Roberts, Celia. 2000. 'Biological behaviour? Hormones, psychology and sex', *NWSA Journal* 12: 1–20.

Rogers, Lesley. 2000. *Sexing the Brain*. London: Phoenix.

Roper, Michael. 1994. *Masculinity and the British Organization Man since 1945*. Oxford: Oxford University Press.

Rosenberg, Rosalind. 1982. *Beyond Separate Spheres: Intellectual Roots of Modern Feminism*. New Haven: Yale University Press.

Rowbotham, Sheila. 1969. *Women's Liberation and the New Politics*. Nottingham: Spokesman.

Rubin, Gayle. 1975. 'The traffic in women: notes on the "political economy" of sex', pp. 157–210 in R. R. Reiter, ed., *Toward an Anthropology of Woman*. New York: Monthly Review.

Rubin, Henry. 2003. *Self-Made Men: Identity and Embodiment among Transsexual Men*. USA: Vanderbilt University Press.

SAHAJ, SAHAYOG and TATHAPI. 2005. *Working With Men on Gender, Sexuality, Violence & Health: Trainer's Manual*. Alkapuri: Vadodara.

Sahlins, Marshall. 1977. *The Use and Abuse of Biology: An Anthropological Critique of Sociobiology*. London: Tavistock.

Sartre, Jean-Paul. 1968. *Search for a Method*, trans. H. Barnes. New York: Vintage.

Sawyer, Jack. [1970] 1974. 'On male liberation', pp. 170–3 in J. H. Peck and J. Sawyer, eds., *Men and Masculinity*. Englewood Cliffs, NJ: Prentice-Hall.

Schofield, T., R. Connell, L. Walker, J. Wood and D. Butland. 2000. 'Understanding men's health: a gender relations approach to masculinity, health and illness', *Journal of American College Health* 48: 247–56.

Schools Commission (Australia). 1975. *Girls, School and Society*. Canberra: Schools Commission.

Schreiner, Olive. [1911] 1978. *Woman and Labour*. London: Virago.

Scott, Joan W. 1986. 'Gender: a useful category of historical analysis', *American Historical Review* 91, 5: 1053–75.

Segal, Lynne. 1994. *Straight Sex: Rethinking the Politics of Pleasure*. Berkeley: University of California Press.

Seifert, Ruth. 1993. *Individualisierungsprozesse, Geschlechterverhältnisse und die soziale Konstruktion des Soldaten*. Munich: Sozialwissenschaftliches Institut der Bundeswehr.

Severiens, Sabine, and Geer ten Dam. 1998. 'A multi-level analysis of gender differences in learning orientations', *British Journal of Educational Psychology* 68: 595–608.

Shen, Zhi. 1987. 'Development of Women's Studies – the Chinese way. Sidelights of the National Symposium on Theoretical Studies on Women', *Chinese Sociology and Anthropology* 20: 18–25.

Sideris, Tina. 2005. ' "You have to change and you don't know how!": contesting what it means to be a man in a rural area of South Africa', pp. 111–37 in Graeme Reid and Liz Walker, eds., *Men Behaving Differently*. Cape Town: Double Storey Books.

Silber, Irina Carlota. 2004. 'Mothers/fighters/citizens: violence and disillusionment in post-war El Salvador', *Gender and History* 16: 561–87.

Simon-Kumar, Rachael. 2004. 'Negotiating emancipation: the public sphere and gender critiques of neo-liberal development', *International Feminist Journal of Politics* 6: 485–506.

Sinclair-Webb, Emma. 2000. 'Our Bülent is now a commando: military service and manhood in Turkey', pp. 65–92 in Mai Ghoussoub and Emma Sinclair-Webb, eds., *Imagined Masculinities: Male Identity and Culture in the Modern Middle East*. London: Saqi Books.

Smiler, Andrew P. 2004. 'Thirty years after the discovery of gender: psychological concepts and measures of masculinity', *Sex Roles* 50: 15–26.

Spivak, Gayatri Chakravorty. 1988. *In Other Worlds: Essays in Cultural Politics*. New York: Routledge.

1999. *A Critique of Postcolonial Reason: Toward a History of the Vanishing Present*. Cambridge, Mass.: Harvard University Press.

Stacey, Judith. 1983. *Patriarchy and Socialist Revolution in China*. Berkeley: University of California Press.

Steele, Valerie. 1996. *Fetish: Fashion, Sex and Power*. New York: Oxford University Press.

Stienstra, Deborah. 2000. 'Dancing resistance from Rio to Beijing: transnational women's organizing and United Nations conferences, 1992–6', pp. 209–24 in M. H. Marchand and A. S. Runyan, eds., *Gender and Global Restructuring: Sightings, Sites and Resistances*. London: Routledge.

Stobbe, Lineke. 2005. 'Doing machismo: legitimating speech acts as a selection discourse', *Gender, Work & Organization* 12: 105–23.

Stockholm International Peace Research Institute. 2008. *SIPRI Yearbook 2008*. Oxford: Oxford University Press.

Stoller, Robert J. 1968. *Sex and Gender*, vol. I: *On the Development of Masculinity and Femininity*. London: Hogarth Press.

Strathern, Marilyn. 1978. 'The achievement of sex: paradoxes in Hagen gender-thinking', pp. 171–202 in E. Schwimmer, ed., *The Yearbook of Symbolic Anthropology*. London: Hurst.

Stryker, Susan, and Stephen Whittle, eds. 2006. *The Transgender Studies Reader*. New York: Routledge.

Taga Futoshi. 2007. 'The trends of discourse on fatherhood and father's conflict in Japan'. Paper presented at 15th biennial conference of Japanese Studies Association of Australia, Canberra, July 2007.

Tanaka, Kazuko. 1977. *A Short History of the Women's Movement in Modern Japan*, 3rd edition. Japan: Femintern Press.

Temkina, Anna. 2008. *Sexual Life of Women: Between Subordination and Freedom*. St Petersburg: European University at St Petersburg.

Tharu, Susie, and Tejaswini Niranjana. 1996. 'Problems for a contemporary theory of gender', pp. 232–60 in *Subaltern Studies*, vol. IX. Delhi: Oxford University Press.

Theberge, Nancy. 1991. 'Reflections on the body in the sociology of sport', *Quest* 43: 123–34.

Thorne, Barrie. 1993. *Gender Play: Girls and Boys in School*. New Brunswick: Rutgers University Press.

Tienari, Janne, Anne-Marie Søderberg, Charlotte Holgersson and Eero Vaara. 2005. 'Gender and national identity constructions in the cross-border merger context', *Gender, Work & Organization* 12: 217–41.

Tinsman, Heidi. 2000. 'Reviving feminist materialism: gender and neoliberalism in Pinochet's Chile', *Signs* 26: 145–88.

Tohidi, Nayereh. 1991. 'Gender and Islamic fundamentalism: feminist politics in Iran', pp. 251–65 in C. T. Mohanty, A. Russo and L. Torres, eds., *Third World Women and the Politics of Feminism*. Bloomington: Indiana University Press.

Tomsen, Stephen. 1998. ' "He had to be a poofter or something": violence, male honour and heterosexual panic', *Journal of Interdisciplinary Gender Studies* 3, 2: 44–57.

Torres, Lourdes. 1991. 'The construction of the self in U.S. Latina biographies', pp. 271–87 in C. T. Mohanty, A. Russo and L. Torres, eds., *Third World Women and the Politics of Feminism*. Bloomington: Indiana University Press.

Troiden, Richard R. 1989. 'The formation of homosexual identities', *Journal of Homosexuality* 17: 43–73.

Twenge, Jean M. 1997. 'Changes in masculine and feminine traits over time: a meta-analysis', *Sex Roles* 36: 305–25.

United Nations Development Programme. 2007. *Human Development Report 2007/2008*. New York: Palgrave Macmillan.

Vaerting, Mathilde [writing as Mathilde and Mathias Vaerting]. [1921] 1981. *The Dominant Sex: A Study in the Sociology of Sex Differentiation*. Westport, Conn.: Hyperion.

Valdés, Teresa, ed. 2001. *El Indice de Compromiso Cumplido – ICC: una estrategía para el control ciudadano de la equidad de género*. Santiago: FLACSO.

Valdés, Teresa, and Enrique Gomáriz. 1995. *Latin American Women: Compared Figures*. Santiago: Instituto de la Mujer and FLACSO.

Vickers, Jill. 1994. 'Notes toward a political theory of sex and power', pp. 174–93 in H. L. Radtke and J. S. Henderikus, eds., *Power/Gender*. London: Sage.

Waetjen, Thembisa. 2004. *Workers and Warriors: Masculinity and the Struggle for Nation in South Africa*. Urbana: University of Illinois Press.

Waetjen, Thembisa, and Gerhard Maré. 2001. ' "Men amongst men": masculinity and Zulu nationalism in the 1980s', pp. 195–206 in R. Morrell, ed., *Changing Men in Southern Africa*. London: Zed Books.

Wajcman, Judy. 1999. *Managing like a Man: Women and Men in Corporate Management*. Cambridge: Polity, and Sydney: Allen & Unwin.

Walby, Sylvia. 1990. *Theorizing Patriarchy*. Oxford: Basil Blackwell.

1997. *Gender Transformations*. London: Routledge.

Walby, Sylvia, and Jonathan Allen. 2004. *Domestic Violence, Sexual Assault and Stalking: Findings from the British Crime Survey*. London: Home Office.

Ward, Lester F. [1883] 1897. *Dynamic Sociology, or Applied Science*. New York: Appleton.

Weedon, Chris. 1987. *Feminist Practice and Poststructuralist Theory*. Oxford: Basil Blackwell.

West, Candace, and Don H. Zimmerman. 1987. 'Doing gender', *Gender and Society* 1: 125–51.

White, Patrick. 1979. *The Twyborn Affair*. London: Cape.

White, Sara C. 2000. ' "Did the Earth move?" The hazards of bringing men and masculinities into gender and development', *IDS Bulletin* 31, 2: 33–41.

Williams, Walter L. 1986. *The Spirit and the Flesh: Sexual Diversity in American Indian Culture*. Boston: Beacon Press.

Wollstonecraft, Mary. [1792] 1975. *Vindication of the Rights of Woman*. Harmondsworth: Penguin.

Xaba, Thokozani. 2001. 'Masculinity and its malcontents: the confrontation between "struggle masculinity" and "post-struggle masculinity" (1990–1997)', pp. 105–24 in R. Morrell, ed., *Changing Men in Southern Africa*. London: Zed Books.

Yeatman, Anna. 1990. *Bureaucrats, Technocrats, Femocrats: Essays on the Contemporary Australian State*. Sydney: Allen & Unwin.

Yuval-Davis, Nira. 1997. *Gender and Nation*. London: Sage.

Zulehner, Paul M., and Rainer Volz. 1998. *Männer im Aufbruch: Wie Deutschlands Männer sich selbst und wie Frauen sie sehen*. Ostfildern: Schwabenverlag.

Index